T A C K

The Young Adult's Guide to Getting In, Succeeding and Influencing Others in the Work World

By Mara Weissmann, Esq. and Harvey Robbins, PhD

outskirtspress
DENVER COLORADO

Tack
The Young Adult's Guide to Getting In, Succeeding and Influencing Others in the Work World
All Rights Reserved.
Copyright © 2015 Mara Weissmann, Esq. and Harvey Robbins, PhD
V4.0

Outskirts Press, Inc.
http://www.outskirtspress.com

ISBN: 978-1-4787-6341-3

Outskirts Press and the "OP" logo are trademarks belonging to Outskirts Press, Inc.

PRINTED IN THE UNITED STATES OF AMERICA

Dedications

Mara

To the men in my life and Mom.

My husband, Richard, you set the bar high and inspire me always.

My sons, Gabriel and Noah, you give me reason to think and feel each day of every month and every month of each year, forever and always.

My brother, Aaron, so often, you are my guiding light.

My dad, your amazing legacy spurs me on in infinite ways.

Mom, thank you for being my biggest cheerleader and for teaching me how to set goals and achieve them.

Harvey

To my wife, Nancy, for her continuous support and to my son, Max, whose tenacity inspired my participation in the writing of this book.

Table of Contents

Introduction – Setting the Scene

From the earliest times, explorers on land or sea have been map-makers. They wanted those who came after to benefit from their experience, to not have to make the same "mistakes" as they had. However, the maps and charts they made were partial—they couldn't travel everywhere—so they filled in the gaps as best they could. There were always areas that remained unexplored and un-explained, and they indicated their lack of knowledge with the statement, "Here be monsters."

As technology developed, these areas of unknown, to a large ex-tent, became known. With satellite imaging, the Internet, and ad-vanced technology, every corner of the globe is now "visible," and we can be lured into a false sense of security, into thinking that the monsters have been eliminated. But that's not so. The long-distance view gives us a map, but that doesn't mean we know the territory, what it is like at ground or sea level.

The same concept applies to the work world. Many explorers came before you and many more will follow. Young adults today grew up with the world just a click of the keypad away, and you want infor-mation quickly. We wrote this book to do just that. We want to give you information quickly, in digestible form, and provide you mentor-ship and the tools for success that took us several decades to learn.

This book continues the exploration of the world—the contempo-rary world of work with its multigenerational workforce. The maps are here to guide the next generations of young people who, we believe, will need exploration tips. They already have some maps and charts made in earlier times; they have heuristics that older generations found useful. But things need to be updated, the current "monsters" identified and tamed. This book provides those maps.

The title of this book, *Tack*, refers to a sailing maneuver by which a vessel turns its bow into the wind so that the sailboat can alter its course or avoid an obstacle. It is the way to sail a boat upwind. We called the book *Tack* because, in the work environment, we are often called upon to change course, alter our strategy, and call upon our teammates to help us steer the course. More often than not, we need to change direction or take a different approach to avoid a conflict or deal with a colleague that may have a different style than our own. Therefore, during our career journey, we all must, at one time or another, tack.

People often use sports metaphors in business. No sport compares to the work world like sailing and sailboat racing.

In sailboat racing, for example, there is usually more than one person against whom you are competing, and teamwork is most important. Racing involves situational tactics, but you also need to have a long-term strategy for the sail, one that is adaptable as conditions change. Boats sailing with the wind coming over the starboard (right) side of the boat are on *starboard tack* and have the right-of-way over boats going the other way. Tactics help you decide, when you're on *port tack* approaching a starboard boat, whether you should cross behind the other boat, or tack so that you're on starboard, too. Tactics also help you decide how to maneuver when a bunch of boats all come together at a particular point. These tactics are heavily influenced by the sailing Rules of the Road.

Like in sailing, you can learn tactics to deal with specific work situations. In business, you use tactics to help customers or clients become aware of your existence, to smooth relationships with unhappy customers or clients, and to form partnerships with other businesses. Business tactics help you navigate the seas of commerce, and while you may not be trying to win at the expense of others, sound business tactics can prevent you from losing.

Strategy

When sailing, sometimes you want to go left, sometimes right, sometimes straight up the middle. It depends on wind conditions, current, and the presence of other vessels on the water, among other factors.

In business, if you don't have a strategy, you have to react to what comes along. If you have a strategy, you can make better decisions about which of the presented options you will choose. Strategy helps you deal with environmental conditions, anticipate the changing conditions, and create contingency plans for when those changes happen.

Equipment

The condition of your sailboat and gear matters. If your hull is not completely smooth, it creates more drag in the water, slowing down your boat speed. If your sails are old and stretched out, they do not generate as much lift, and you don't go as fast. If your rigging is in the wrong place, your crew loses efficiency while maneuvering and you end up behind other boats.

Equipment in sailing is equivalent to your personal equipment—your core self, the left and right hemispheres of your brain, your drive and motivation. It is the traits, natural inclinations, and temperaments you've had since you were born and the identity that you've developed in response to your journey through the external world and your interaction with others.

Environmental Conditions

Unlike the other factors, environmental conditions are completely out of your control. This is important to realize because there is a lot in the work world that is out of your hands. In sailing, you can't control which way the wind blows, which direction it will shift next, or what the underlying current is doing. But you have to consider these factors—the boats that best anticipate changing conditions are those that come out ahead.

What better metaphor for business? Those who have navigated the business waters can intuitively sense when conditions are about to change and can plan for these changes effectively. If you are not aware of the conditions and people around you, and you can't assess how they may affect you and others, you could find yourself in the wrong tack when conditions turn. In business, having a long-term strategy can help you succeed. Think about business moves that set you up for success in the future, consider your competition, and don't get caught up in individual setbacks.

The parallels between sailing and business go on and on. All businesses and all sailboat racers need to excel at teamwork, tactics, strategy, and navigation of environmental conditions to come out ahead.[i]

Why This Book Was Written

The purpose of this book is to help you—a young adult (or someone closely associated with you)—to reduce the unknown, increase your opportunities and success in the work-world arena, and shrink the expectations gap between young adult employees and their employers. We wrote this book to help young adult employees slay the monsters standing in the way of their success and to fill in the unknown with knowledge and skills. We wrote this book to help young adults thrive and excel in the real work world.

Note

The names of clients and others in many of the stories we tell have been changed in order to protect confidentiality. Also, while much of our research pertains to the current generation, Millennials, the advice in this book is for all young adults who are about to enter or who are already in the workplace.

PART 1 –
Getting In

Chapter 1

Hoisting your Sail and Launching Your Boat: Making a Good First Impression

If you do nothing else, you must read this first chapter. This is the personal flotation device (aka life jacket) you are handed on every boat. For now, it seems like just a good piece of advice. Later on in the book, you'll find out why this is an essential part of your work-life survival kit.

Tickets Please!

Sorry, there are no free rides or quick trips down the career navigation course. Careers are built over a lifetime. The best advice (and there is a lot of it in this book) that we can give you is to enjoy the process of building your career. Mara had a client tell her, six months into her first job, that she wanted to go to graduate school and then start a consulting business like Mara's. Mara told her to slow down. Six months into a first job does not make one an expert on anything. Your main goal in the first several years of your career is to gain as much experience and knowledge in your chosen field as possible. There is plenty of time to attain your long-term goals. Remember, some of those objectives are just that: long-term goals.

Along your career journey, demands will be made on you. All kinds of demands. You will need various resources, such as money, but you will also need value: qualifications, certificates, and proof of ability. To navigate the choppy seas ahead, you'll need an old-fashioned sextant to estimate your position, and a knowledge of the tides, the seas, and the oceans that you are likely to be crossing in order to plot the best course. We call that good judgment and an intuitive and analytical way of thinking. And you will need to have a plan for what to do when you encounter the doldrums. We are the creators and navigators of our own careers. Though a lot depends on the organization (Is it successful? Is it a place where people can advance their careers?) and your boss (Is he or she supportive, a mentor who is able to assist in positioning you for success?), no organization or boss can navigate our careers for us. So let's be the captains of our own careers right from the start of our long career journey.

Sailing, particularly racing, is all about teamwork. We counsel many student athletes and help them identify their particular value having been part of a team. More about that later. First, each person has a specific job, with specific responsibilities. One person steers the boat. Another trims the sails to make the boat go fast. Others raise and lower sails at the right moment, and everybody looks out for traffic. Some of the worst mistakes happen when somebody wants or tries to do someone else's job.

Practice helps, as does communication. If everyone knows his or her job, the boat has a better chance of sailing faster and more smoothly. If people are confused about what they're supposed to do or when they're supposed to do it, the likelihood of a mistake or failure rises.

Setting Sail: Starting with the Interview

Job interviews today are a hybrid of skills-based, behavior-based, and situational-based evaluations and inquiries. Employers want to know whether you have technical skills to do the job, but they also want to know about you, your character, how you will perform when presented with a particular situation, and what your past performance suggests about how you will perform in the future.

According to a study by Leadership IQ, 46% of newly hired employees will fail within eighteen months, while only 19% will achieve unequivocal success. But contrary to popular belief, technical skills account for only 11% of why new hires fail; sadly, it's poor attitude that dominates the list—flaws that many managers admit were overlooked during the interview process.[ii]

Our learning from this is critical: in addition to whether you have the technical skills to competently execute a job, employers are evaluating you for your ability to be coached, motivation, temperament, and emotional intelligence (EQ), which is defined by experts as "a person's ability to manage his or her emotions effectively, relate to others, read and adapt to a cultural environment, and influence other people positively."[iii] In the workplace, an employee who demonstrates emotional intelligence can lead, work effectively with others, deal with change, take criticism, and stay positive in the face of adversity. We will talk about emotional intelligence later in this book.

There are hundreds of different questions that one could be asked in a job interview, but we will help you to synthesize the interview process framework. While interview questions come in many different forms, they boil down to five general inquiries:

1. They want to know if you are qualified for the position.
- What are your greatest strengths?
- Do you have experience in this field?
- What do you believe you bring to this job?
- Why should I hire you?

2. They want to know what motivates you.
- What motivates you to put forth your greatest effort?
- Where do you see yourself five years from now?
- What is more important to you, the money or the job?
- What did you like most about your last job?

3. They want to know about the negatives, whether you can be introspective, and whether they can trust you to learn from mistakes and improve on what may not come easily to you.
- Why did you leave your previous job?
- What did you like least about your last supervisor?
- What is your greatest weakness?
- What did you like least about your last job?
- Why have you been unemployed so long?

4. They want to know if you are a good fit: are you a team player, are you able to learn from others, are you adaptable, can you set goals and achieve them, and will you handle yourself in a professional manner.
- What kind of people do you find it hard to work with?
- Tell me about a time when you worked as a member of a team.

- In what kind of environment are you most comfortable?
- Do you prefer to work alone or with others?

5. *They want to know if you really want this job with their company and whether you will be a valued contributor.*
   - What are you looking for in a position?
   - Who else are you interviewing with?
   - Why are you interested in this position?

What do you know about the company?

Your ability to connect with the interviewer and skillfully articulate your responses will be key to your success in the interview process. That is easier said than done. Most people do not like talking about themselves—they see it as bragging or they think the resume should speak for itself.

Bragging about, overstating, or presuming away your qualifications are not winning strategies. This is one moment in your life where it is critical to sell yourself, your value, and your character through noteworthy words, encapsulating descriptions, and memorable stories of your life experiences that convey the essence of you and your strengths—to make yourself stand out.

The bad news is that most adults have an attention span of eight seconds and form first impressions within the first few minutes of meeting someone. The good news is that you have the ability to have the interviewer at "Hello" with a well-prepared response to the first question you will likely be asked: "Tell me about yourself" or "Walk me through your resume." Think of it as a 60-second pitch at a 30,000-foot level about your academic, extracurricular, and work experiences; your strengths; and why you want the job at hand.

A client once said, "I sound like a list of what jobs I had and what tasks I did." To avoid sounding like a list, turn your resume on its flip side and start with the question, "What value did I gain from that position, at that company, doing that job, working with those colleagues?"

Picking the Value Out of What You Have Done

So, how do we pick out the value from what you have done throughout your life experiences?

There are many values or attributes that employers want to see in their applicants and employees, such as leadership, research skills, work ethic, critical thinking, wisdom, perseverance, creativity, and innovation, just to name a few. To assist you in identifying your value, we have identified five key behavioral dimensions that we believe employers want to see in their new hires and existing employees. With some thought, you can identify experiences in your academic, extracurricular, and work experiences that exemplify these attributes and behavioral dimensions. It is precisely these values, attributes, or behavioral dimensions that you need to convey throughout your career, particularly when you apply for a job.

The behavioral dimensions that we believe employers value most highly in their applicants and employees are:

1. Results Orientation
2. Adaptability
3. Team Player/Collaboration
4. Altruism (Giving) and Professionalism
5. Communication

Embodying Five Key Behavioral Dimensions Employers Want to See in Their Candidates and Employees

Together we will learn how to embody these behavioral dimensions by accounting for what they mean and what they don't mean.

1. Results Orientation

When you demonstrate that you are results oriented, you concentrate on what you want to achieve by when and how much it will cost. This means you are able to imagine how things will be when you have gotten there, and that will inform how you get there.

Words that describe a person who is results oriented:

- Industrious
- Tireless
- Gumptious
- Energetic
- Unwearying
- Up-and-coming
- Indefatigable
- Conveys quickness and constancy of action

- Agile
- Diligent
- Able to actively promote an enterprise or endeavor
- Able to build something
- Hardworking
- Drive an outcome
- Risk taker
- Creates and executes
- Curious

Words that describe a person who is not results oriented:
- Theoretical
- Not focused
- Follower mentality
- Lazy
- Waster of time
- Puts up barriers to getting things done
- Distracted by others

2. Adaptability

Because no outcome is ever quite what you wanted or expected, you have to be alert to what is happening during the process of getting to the end result and either steer things back on track or else decide that something better is happening and adjust your plans accordingly.

Words that describe a person with positive flexibility (willingness to be adaptable):

- Patient
- Enduring
- Possesses fortitude
- Gutsy
- Consumed with vitality
- Pliant
- Vision attentive
- Competent
- Able to self-correct
- Resilient

Words that describe a person with positive versatility (ability to be adaptable):

- Confident
- Tolerant
- Empathic
- Positive
- Respectful of others
- Resourceful

Words that describe a person without flexibility (willingness to be adaptable):

- Rigid
- Unhealthily competitive with others
- Discontent
- Unapproachable

Words that describe a person without versatility (ability to be adaptable):

- Subjective
- Blunt
- Resistant to change
- Myopic
- Unreasonable risk taker

3. Team Player/Collaboration

If you are working for someone else, then you are, by definition, part of a team, and that affects the way you behave. You have to share information and appreciate the contributions of others, rather than going it alone or claiming glory for your own individual achievements. Think about being a part of a sports team or being in the band or orchestra or on stage in a play or musical. You play your individual position, instrument, or role, but you are part of the greater whole.

Words that describe a person who collaborates:

- Works well with others for a common purpose or outcome
- Knows how to integrate one's individual role with the goals of the team

Words that describe a person who does not work well in a team and cannot collaborate:

- Excessive competitor
- Unable to provide individual recognition to others
- Hyperactive ego
- Lacks effort
- Lacks synergy among individual efforts
- Unable to equitably divide responsibility
- Poor communicator

4. Altruism (Giving) and Professionalism

This is about going the extra mile in order to achieve organizational or group outcomes—and that includes holding the team together so that they are functioning and achieving well. As a representative of the organization, you will conform to their standards and guidelines, thus acquiring respect from others. This concept is about demonstrating how you roll up your sleeves, jump into the trenches, and go full throttle (i.e., work hard). Particularly in the first few years of your career, you should not be focused on what you are getting (other than a paycheck, an occasional performance review, and a place to hang your hat and coat). Ask yourself what you can do for your company instead of what your company can do for you. (Sound familiar? Thank you, Mr. President). This Ted Goff cartoon best describes the concept of altruism:

© 2009 Ted Goff

"Where do I see myself in five years? Helping you achieve greatness, of course."

Words that describe a person who is altruistic and professional:

- Self-aware and self-regulating
- Reads others (empathy)
- Able to learn from mistakes
- Considerate
- Accommodating
- Giving
- Generous
- Friendly
- Cooperative
- Unselfish
- All-hands-on-deck mentality
- Obliging

Words that describe a person who is not altruistic and professional:

- Self-interested
- Disobliging
- Greedy
- Selfish
- Alienating
- Mean
- Disrespectful
- Egoistic
- Arrogant
- Supercilious
- Condescending
- Lacks empathy
- Narcissistic: an individual who is excessively preoccupied with issues of personal adequacy, power, prestige, and vanity

5. Communication

Underpinning all of these attributes is the ability and willingness to communicate with others at all levels, both formally and informally, orally and in writing. Communication has two aspects: what you communicate to others and how you receive information directed at you. The latter is called active listening.

Words that describe a person who is a good communicator:

- Good one-on-one verbal language skills

- Good writing skills
- Good presentation skills
- Able to convey thoughts, opinions, and suggestions
- Questions and provides answers in an appropriate and professional manner
- Good listening skills
- Shares information
- Goes on a listening tour – people like to hear themselves speak
- Lets the other person know what you heard them say even when you do not agree with the content
- Aware of body language
- Narrates life – communicating where you are in the process
- Gives and receives feedback in a mature manner
- Speaks with substance

Words that describe a person who is not a good communicator:

- Sarcastic
- Blames others
- Puts down others
- Demanding
- Passive aggressive
- Scapegoating
- Defensive
- Counterattacks
- Blames
- Escalates emotions
- Promotes melodrama
- Stirs the pot

- Imposes guilt
- Spins your head
- Lectures

Exercise #1

- Sit with your resume and identify all the experiences you have had that elicit positive behavioral dimensions or value.
- Think about how others perceive you and the feedback you have gotten from your colleagues or friends. If you possess any of the negative behaviors, look inward and think about what you may want to change. The ability to do this will be important as you progress through your career, as some of the negative behaviors will surface time and again.
- Think about the positive dimensions and values you possess and embody them. Identify the experiences that best exemplify these dimensions and values. Begin to look at your life experiences in a story-telling kind of way.

For example, if you are applying for a job in consulting and you worked one summer in your local diner as a waiter, the value gained from that job—understanding the importance of customer or client service—is a key skillset and value for any consulting job. Employers want to hear you articulate a story about how you learned about the value of client service skills as opposed to the mere fact that you worked for a drive-in, diner, or dive waiting tables. You will have a greater opportunity to better know yourself in the next chapter.

Another example is the student athlete. Student athletes possess many attributes that are valuable to a company and many companies know this and look for student athletes to fill their ranks. But do not assume that the interviewer knows that you have these qualities merely because varsity lacrosse is on your resume. You need to convey your value to the interviewer. Forbes featured a great article titled "Why You Should Fill Your Company With 'Athletes'"[iv] that lists the following attributes of athletes:

- "They have the drive to practice a task rigorously, relentlessly, and even in the midst of failure until they succeed. Athletes are tenacious—they seldom or never give up. They also have a strong work ethic and the ability to respect and deal with the inevitable issues of temporary pain (along with the intuition to know when the cause of the pain is an issue too serious to ignore).
- Athletes achieve their goals. If one avenue is blocked, they find another path to success. If their physical strength has given out, they learn to work smarter, not harder. As they learn to become more effective, they become more efficient.
- Athletes develop new skills. Even though an athlete is highly specialized at certain skills, such as speed, blocking, or hand-eye coordination, they are also good at adapting to scenarios that call for cross-functional skills.
- Athletes are exceptional entrepreneurs. As [businesses] consider new hires, [they] will likely discover that business athletes are often former (or current) entrepreneurs. Whereas people from large corporate environments may tend to be specialized in their skills and single-minded in their ob-

jectives, a business athlete is equipped to see the bigger vision of all that goes into making a company thrive. They can think strategically and are tuned in to the 'big picture' and the long-term goals. They also know how to put the strategy into action.

- Athletes strive for balance. Too much junk food and too little sleep will not contribute to a healthy company or a winning performance. Their bodies must be strong and in good condition, so athletes understand that they can't cheat the system for long and expect positive results. A true business athlete will respect the laws of balance in energy, health, sleep, and nutrition (as well as the business corollaries) that will allow them to succeed and to do so not only in the present but for the long term as well.

- Athletes work well with partners and in teams. Athletes know how to leverage the unique and complementary strengths of each member of their team. They know that cutting down a teammate or disrespecting a partner will only contribute to an organization's demise. In fact, an athlete will typically put the needs of the team or a partner on equal par or even ahead of their own needs."[v]

Have the Interviewer at "Hello" with a Well-Designed Elevator Speech

The first question that you will be asked in an interview is "Tell me about yourself" or "Walk me through your resume." The answer necessitates you having a well-constructed elevator pitch.

What is an elevator pitch and why is it important? An elevator pitch, elevator speech, or elevator statement is a short summary used to quickly and simply define who you are: your pedigree, industry skills and relevance, communication skills, leadership qualities and problem solving abilities, what is important to you, and your value proposition.

The name "elevator pitch" reflects the idea that it should be possible to deliver the summary in the time span of an elevator ride. If you found yourself in the elevator at the ground floor with the CEO of the company for which you work, and he or she said, "Tell me about yourself," your elevator pitch would be your answer. It should be no longer than sixty seconds. If the conversation inside the elevator in those seconds is interesting and valuable, the conversation will continue after the elevator ride.

Having interviewed hundreds and hundreds of people in our careers, we can tell you that even experienced adults have difficulty answering, "Tell me about yourself." We have heard answers such as, "Gee, where do I begin?" and "That's a tough question." Those folks, right from the start, are rejected for the job.

First impressions go a long way. If you do not want to be tossed overboard when you are asked, "Tell me about yourself," you must sound prepared, organized, and confident. You have to be succinct, particularly since an adult's attention span is typically eight seconds long.

- Your aim is to "sell" the interviewer something different, perhaps even something they hadn't considered important or on their list of desirable qualities. It should, of course, have some relevance to the job.

The problem here is that unless the listener's attention is grabbed in the first few seconds, they switch off. The interviewer craves novelty. If you start with a long preamble, which says nothing much, then the interviewer's thoughts will drift out to sea instead of listening to you.

How do you get their attention?

- Have a hook. In the first ten seconds, give your audience a reason to want to listen for the next half hour.
- Pitch yourself, not your ideas. Pitch what YOU can offer the institution.
- Highlight a strong interest in the opportunity and the skills that are most important to your success on the job. Highlight who you are: your pedigree; industry skills relevance; communication, leadership, and problem-solving skills; what is important to you; and the impact you believe that you will have.
- Convey interest in learning and being intellectually curious. If you can, incorporate what you know about their career.
- Express your passions and how they might relate to a career at the company.
- Exude confidence and enthusiasm.

Your purpose is to pitch yourself and what YOU can offer the institution through the value you have created from your academic, extracurricular, and work experiences.

- If there is anything you need to do, it is this: translate your experiences into value-added, applied skills about which you will speak during your elevator pitch and an interview.

In other words, you do not want your elevator pitch to sound like a laundry list of tasks you did when describing your jobs, your classes, or your overall resume.

Example of an elevator pitch:

"I am a senior at XYZ College where I am majoring in communications. I have a 3.8 GPA evidencing my strong work ethic and drive. I am a varsity squash player, which has taught me teamwork; how to be self-motivated, goal focused, and resilient; and how to manage my time effectively. I have had internships in the media, entertainment, and healthcare industries and have acquired valuable skills such as attention to detail, client service, analysis of complex information, and the synthesis of that information into understandable terms. I am completely open to being trained, I am adaptable, and I collaborate well with others and attain the goals I set for myself. I am interested in [*x* position at *y* company] because you have a reputation of hiring top college graduates and training them in the field of media planning and strategy, you have clients in the mid-market which allows you to develop strong, partnering relationships with your clients, and I would be privileged to work with your team."

In the interview, you will be required to provide more detailed examples of these value-added applied skills you acquired. Young adults, generally speaking, have a difficult time translating their accomplishments and experiences into value that employers want to see in their candidates.

We believe it is always important in life to put yourself in the shoes of others. So let's look at the situation from the interviewer's perspective. Interviewing candidates for jobs is not an exact science. It requires a lot of practice and preparation on the part of the interviewer. It also requires of the interviewer the skill to predict the future, the ability to sum up another person based on a limited knowledge of them, the ability to "see behind the mask" that the interview situation inevitably invokes, and the ability to read between the lines to ascertain the presence or absence of certain desirable characteristics and behaviors that are important in the job. These are tough requirements, which is why a company will often resort to paper-and-pencil tests, profiling questionnaires, and so on. Perhaps the best way of finding out if someone is suitable for a particular job is to get them to do the job for a while and see how they do. This is not always feasible but it is why young adults often find themselves in internships. So, given the challenges here, how do you make the best of it—how do you convey your value and get yourself hired?

The first step is to get to know yourself better. Find out the metrics an organization is likely to use and see how you match up. Then, look at the job description or google a model job description of the particular position that you are seeking (or google "characteristics of a good [financial analyst]") and link up your value with the attributes of a person who holds that desired position or the requirements of that position. The most critical question you can answer is: what is the value I bring to the table? Find the value in the job you had, the tasks you did, and the people with whom you worked.

The framework you need to focus on in the course of your interview is this:

- *Characteristics*: who and what you are
- *Behaviors*: what you do and how you think vis-à-vis others – capability and empathy
- *Values*: your guiding principles – how you relate to the world of work, in terms of ethics, giving back
- *Creativity*: your imagination, ability to think outside the box and problem solve.

Even if there are no explicit questions clearly delineated like this, there will still be questions that cover these aspects of you. And you can always work in your five key values when they ask you, "Is there anything that we haven't talked about that I should know about you?" Hit the interviewer with this: "I believe that my strengths are that I set personal and professional goals and achieve them; I am adaptable; I stand ready, willing, and able to work hard and learn; I am a good team player and communicate well."

Telling a Story that Conveys Your Value

A successful interview isn't a cross examination; it's a conversation. If you want to break out of the question/answer ping-pong match, you should aim to sprinkle in some interesting information about yourself in the shape of stories.

By using stories, you will:

- Appeal to the human mind.
- Be remembered.
- Create a strong connection with the listener.
- Demonstrate your communication skills.

So exactly how do you tell a story? First, listen to the questions and apply the right story about your past experience. Sell yourself by describing what actions you took, what skills you used, and what results you achieved. Put the focus on the employer and their needs as opposed to your ego. The STAR method is a structured manner of responding to a behavioral-based interview question by discussing the specific situation, task, action, and result of the situation you are describing.

- *Situation*: Describe the situation that you were in or the task that you needed to accomplish. You must describe a specific event or situation, not a generalized description of what you have done in the past. Be sure to give enough detail for the interviewer to understand. This situation can be from a previous job, from a volunteer experience, or any relevant event.

- *Task*: What goal were you working toward?
- *Action*: Describe the actions you took to address the situation with an appropriate amount of detail and keep the focus on *you*. What specific steps did you take and what was your particular contribution? Be careful that you don't describe what the team or group did when talking about a project, but what you actually did. Use the word "I," not "we" when describing actions.
- *Result*: Describe the outcome of your actions and don't be shy about taking credit for your behavior. What happened? How did the event end? What did you accomplish? What did you learn? Make sure your answer contains multiple positive results.

Exercise #2

Outcome Driven – Results Oriented

- Prepare a story demonstrating your ability to build something from beginning to end.

Adaptable

- Prepare a story demonstrating a time when you changed your behavior to accommodate someone else, which in turn increased your communication and helped build relationships with other people.
- Prepare a story about how you resolved a conflict, how you dealt with a massive blow and bounced back, and how you

coped under pressure.

Team Player/Collaborator

- Prepare a story for how you helped the team to achieve a great goal or how you increased the team spirit so that nobody has left that team since.

Altruistic and Professional

- Prepare a story demonstrating how you helped someone without expecting anything in return.
- Prepare a story demonstrating how you can deal with the negatives and turn them into something positive.

Communicator

- Prepare a story demonstrating how you successfully communicated a situation so that the other person came around to seeing your point of view.

Don't Forget the Likeability Factor

Before you get nervous at the prospect of sitting across a desk and answering tough questions, remember that an interview is just a personal interaction between two individuals and depends a lot on how well you and the interviewer connect. Ask any number of recruiters what really made them choose one candidate over the other, especially when they all had very similar qualifications and skills sets, and the most common answer is, "There was a good cultural fit," or a more honest answer, "We liked that candidate better."

1. *Be friendly*, tilt your head ever so slightly, and smile often. Friendliness is a basic element of likeability. Effortlessly smile when you first meet the interviewer. An endearing smile quickly breaks the ice, makes you seem attractive and confident, and transmits positive feelings. As a matter of fact, people who smile more are more likely to get hired and promoted. A good handshake immediately following a smile helps to make a great first impression. The firm but not aggressive handshake will convey that you are confident, social, and professional before you utter your first word.

2. *Develop stories* about your experiences to convey your value, key strengths, and behavioral dimensions. Stories give you the opportunity to create an emotional rapport with the interviewer and will help make you memorable and likeable.

3. *Be enthusiastic* and express passion about your accomplishments and experiences.

Maintain a pleasant expression and an open attitude that tells the interviewer you are happy doing what you do. Enthusiasm means sitting up straight and making eye contact with the person whose questions you are answering and leaning forward in your chair with your feet firmly on the floor. Remember to keep your arms at your sides, or use them to make friendly, conversational gestures. And project your passion in your voice when conversing.

4. ***Be giving***. Remember the behavioral dimension, altruism? We counsel you to share how you roll up your sleeves, jump into the trenches, add value, and go full throttle (aka work hard) for the first years of your career. Find out as much as you can about the job you will be expected to do before you go to interview. This will help you frame your answers on what you can do for the company. Be ready with some ideas on how you can contribute to the organization and even take a mock project with you if you can. This will help the interviewer see how eager you are, how you can add value, and how you can fit in. Always focus on what you can give.

5. ***Be humble***. Project confidence without going overboard or being arrogant.

The secret to being likeable in interviews is to find that fine balance between confidence and humility. Initiate the discussion using quantifiable accomplishments from the past to explain your vantage point. Back up every statement with facts and statistics to validate what you are saying. By staying humble, you can turn the interview into a pleasant dialogue between two interesting people. Employers like to hire someone whose company they enjoy.

6. ***Be honest and sincere*** and exude trust. Be sure that what you say is based on facts and do not add on skills you may not possess and duties you may not have handled. If you are asked a question that you do not have an answer to, admit your lack of knowledge honestly while expressing that you are keen to learn more on the subject. This will help to build trust. If you are sincere in what you say, it will reflect in your conduct and tone of voice. For example, if a person is being interviewed for a sales position, a typical question may be "What is your selling style?" A good answer is this:

> "To begin the sale I try to find common ground on a personal level. I make friends with my customer before I ever start to talk business. I believe that friendship is the basis for open communication: open talk, laughter, sharing stories, finding solid common ground. I establish rapport with them and communicate conversationally, leading to a relaxed atmosphere and open communication. The conversation is natural."

Nothing Like Preparation

The more information you have about a prospective employer, the better prepared you will be during the interview. You need to know about the organization's products or services, trends, and employment requirements. You should also look at the biography or LinkedIn bio of the people with whom you will be interviewing if you know the names ahead of time. This is vital for interview preparation.

Prepare thoughtful questions to ask the interviewer. These are questions that you cannot obtain the answers to in your own thorough research.

Whether your interview is in person or by telephone or Skype, your level of preparation must be the same. Remote interviews via telephone or Skype are becoming more popular, particularly for the first round. With a telephone interview, you should have your resume in front of you as well as your elevator pitch and notes covering your behavioral dimensions that you wish to convey. Practicing your pitch and stories conveying your strengths as part of your preparation before your interview will cause you to sound more natural as opposed to sounding like you are reading off a script. One other tip for a telephone interview: stand up and take the call. Your voice will project greater strength than if you take the call sitting down. A Skype interview is more tricky because you cannot be looking down at and reading your notes during your interview. Eye contact with the interviewer is critical. With a Skype interview, you must be certain where the camera is in order to make purposeful eye contact. A small post-it with key words on it that depict your strengths may be helpful to you during your Skype interview as long as it is not visible to the interviewer.

All interviews should be followed up immediately with a personalized thank you note to all of the individuals with whom you interviewed, whether it is an in-person interview or a telephone or Skype interview. The thank you note should be in email form in order to get it in the hands of the interviewers prior to their making a decision on your candidacy.

PART 2 –
Behaviors for Success

Chapter 2

Knowing the Navigable Waters and Lines and Plotting the Course

There are approximately 76 million people that compose the generation born between 1980– 2000—the Gen Y, also known as the Millennial generation. About 36% of those young adults are currently in or about to join the workforce. By 2020, nearly half (46%) of all US workers will be Millennials. Let us introduce you to a few of them.

Chrissie sent an email to a prospective employer. The salutation began: "Dead Mr. Warner." Not only did she not get the job, she was admonished by Mr. Warner and told never to apply to his company again.

Chelsea broke down and cried in an interview for an HR internship when she was asked behavioral-based questions that she simply could not answer. She got the job because her boss told her that he thought she needed a mentor.

Marissa worked for a media company for two years and was a good but not outstanding employee. She wanted to be promoted to supervisor. She sat down in the HR Director's office, curled her feet under her bottom, leaned on the armrest of the chair, and whined, "I wanna be a supervisor.

Everyone else around here is getting promoted. I have been here two years, and I think I deserve to be a supervisor." She did not get promoted.

Jake, a star candidate, was hired by a major bank right out of his elite liberal arts college. Within the first month, he disregarded working hours, showed a lack of urgency in client matters, and told a senior coworker that he probably will follow his ex-girlfriend to Arizona where she accepted a job. Six months later, Jake quit that job after the partners mentored him and sponsored him for his Series 7, which he took and passed on the bank's dime. He told the partners the office was not social enough for him.

Erin graduated university last May and landed a full-time paid internship at a PR firm. Every time she had a session with Mara, she informed Mara that she is "very good at her job." Three months after she started her first full-time job, she called Mara and said she was at a "crossroads in her career."

George was directed in a mock interview to, "Tell me about yourself." He responded, "Neh, I don't feel like it" and then laughed.

These are real-life stories of young adults. If, for a moment, you think that these students are losers, they are not. They are ambitious, accomplished, and sociable students with high GPAs attending or graduated from the most respected colleges and universities in the country. They have never failed at anything in their lives. Just to be fair and present both sides, in case you want a sneak preview of what some young adults today are thinking, one blogger wrote:

> "What other option do [employers] have? We are hardworking and utilize tools to get the job done. But we don't want to work more than forty hours a week, and we want to wear clothes that are comfortable. We want to be able to spice up the dull workday by listening to our iTunes. If corporate America doesn't like that, too bad."[vi]

The motivators that drive Millennials to succeed are different than their predecessors. The tools in this book capitalize on young adults' ability to absorb information and their desire to be innovative and mentored, their ambition to be leaders and make a difference, and their preference for immediacy and transparency.

Understanding the Multiple Generations in the Workplace

Traditionalists are the oldest generation in the workplace, born 1930–1945. They are very socially and fiscally conservative. Traditionalists fear that they will be replaced by younger generations. Many are still in the workforce because they enjoy working, but some are there for financial reasons. Their life experience gives them a lot to offer.

Baby Boomers are now one of the older generations at work, born 1946–1964. They were born during the booming, optimistic times post World War II. They value hard work and long hours as the means to success, and this work ethic is extremely important to them. Boomers need to be noticed for their hard work. When dealing with other generations, Boomers need to make sure they are very upfront and specific with their instructions.

Generation Xers, born 1965–1979, were raised by Baby Boomers who worked long hours and were the first generation to have widespread divorce. Therefore, Generation Xers are very independent and dislike rigid schedules. They value being efficient and getting work done quickly. They have more balance between their social and work lives than their predecessors and they usher in a more creative, open workplace.

The Millennials were born between 1980 and 2000. Millennials are the first generation to grow up with advanced technologies and, therefore, are very comfortable with technology in every aspect of their lives. Millennials also tend to be opinionated but are very creative and expect to be challenged.

Treating each generation with understanding and respect is the first step in positive relationships between generations. Each generation has a lot to offer and, when the generations work together, their diversity makes for a much more productive and interesting workplace.

Are there differences or similarities among the generations in the workplace?

The concept of fewer differences and more similarities among the generations was the subject of a white paper in 2011 by Professor Marion White who is a Director of UNC's Executive Development Program. Her thesis was that, while there are some tensions among the generations, the generation gap has been overly exaggerated in the popular press and the generations actually have more in common than previously thought.

Those similarities are the need to be respected, feel valued, be connected through collaboration, and have a sense of autonomy, as well as a desire to work on challenging projects, have a competitive salary, have opportunities for advancement and growth in jobs, and have work-life balance. Dr. White cited several studies to support her thesis.[vii] That was in 2011.

They Are Talking About *You*

In 2013, there were too many major publication headlines highlighting the significant issues that young adults, namely Millennials, face in workplaces today to list them all, but here are a few:

- "How College Students Think They Are More Special than EVER"[viii]
- "Bosses say 'Pick Up the Phone'"[ix]
- "Are Millennials Cut Out for this Job Market?"[x]
- "Wanted: Millennials Who Know How to Interview"[xi]

- "Millennials are the Most Stressed-Out Generation"[xii]
- "Generation ME, ME, ME"[xiii]
- "How Millennials Can Survive this Economy"[xiv]
- "Need a Job? Invent It"[xv]
- "How to Get a Job with a Philosophy Degree"[xvi]
- "Seeing Narcissists Everywhere" [xvii]
- "How I Hire: 6 Ways I Find and Hire Hardworking Millennials"[xviii]
- "Losing is Good for You"[xix]
- "Should You Bring Mom and Dad to the Office?"[xx]
- "Why Generation Y'ers are Unhappy"[xxi]
- "Just Graduated, and Fumbling Through a First Job"[xxii]
- "Hiding From Scary Ideas: Do Students Really Need Cookies and Play-Doh to Deal with the Trauma of Listening to Unpopular Opinions?"[xxiii]

We can debate whether the differences are fewer than the similarities or whether the differences are wreaking havoc in the workplace but it seems clear that, to quote our favorite space movie, *Apollo 13*, "Houston, we have a problem." We are here to promote some solutions. So much has been written about how to help businesses and managers accommodate young adults entering the workforce. However, not much has been done to help mentor, coach, and communicate with young adults—a "how-to" rubric, if you will. How to do your job beyond the job description; how to develop your intuition/right-brain thinking; how to adapt to long established business cultures; how to step into the shoes of and empathize with others; how to develop a client/customer service mentality; how to adapt to different people with different social styles; how to accept that your boss's career or your client's needs more often than not come first; how to be professional; how to act and react without emotion and drama in real work-life settings; how to understand the expectations others have and how to manage one's own expectations; how careers develop over a lifetime and are in your hands and not in the hands of the company or a boss; how to understand that the one with the most meaningful connections wins; and how to influence others in a positive way that drives desired outcomes.

Young adults today are smart and possibly the best-educated generation. Imagine, though, if you were cognitively smarter about people and the work-world landscape and more clinically insightful about yourselves and others. Imagine further that you were more psychologically equipped to drive positive outcomes (the ones *you* want) and face the challenges of the real world and to deal effectively with the different personalities that make up that world. And, imagine if you got all this before you came out of the real-life/work-world gate. And then imagine phoning home to highlight your successes instead of what those headlines depict you currently doing, which is complaining about your unhappiness and defeat, being repulsed by desk jobs, or being a narcissist. It's an awesome thought that you can be equipped with real-life skills to provide you with self-esteem based on real-life experiences.

We will explore and understand how you have been raised, parented, and educated; what your work and career expectations are; and what the workplace's expectations are for you. We will then explore what we can do for you to help you bridge the expectations gap.

What the Research Tells Us About How *You* Have Been Raised

The research, which, admittedly, consists of broad generalizations based on evidence and data, tells us that you have come of age in a child-focused world. You have been raised having structured, activity-filled, instruction-filled, and lesson-filled lives. Your parents are highly competitive and have experienced a challenging, methodical climb in their jobs and careers, having worked long hours with increasing pressures.

In fact, a wonderful cartoon by Ted Goff depicts this concept well:

"What are all you people doing on my road to success?"

Your parents placed a high priority on your success in all you do and in your getting ahead. Having raised you during an era of the most violent acts of their time, your parents felt a need to be protective and shelter you from failure, instinctually wanting to protect you from harm, pain, and hardship.

You, on the other hand, grew up wired. You're smart and discerning and are open, eager, and responsive to challenges. You value your leisure time and believe that technology eliminates much of the need for face-to-face meetings.[xxiv]

What the Research Tells Us About How *You* Have Been Educated

Millennials have grown up wired—plugged in—but you don't want to be plugged into a life that is predetermined. You experienced the development of the digital camera, social media, and YouTube. You want to create your own life and pathway for doing things. That creativity and passion is very personal to you and you desire to make a difference. Your generation is in search of meaning in your chosen work and life. Information is instantaneous and at your fingertips.

Jean Twenge, PhD, is one of the leading expert psychologists in the area of generational differences and has done the most cross-generational, over-time data analysis of anyone in the field. Her conclusion, after comparing decades of personality test results, is that the younger generations are increasingly entitled, self-obsessed, and unprepared for the realities of adult life.[xxv] In her well-known book on the subject, *Generation Me*,[xxvi] and her second book *The Narcissism Epidemic*,[xxvii] Dr. Twenge presented data showing generational increases in self-esteem, assertiveness, self-importance, narcissism, and high expectations.

Not surprisingly, her research and conclusions are the subject of criticism. While calling you a generation of narcissists is, in our opinion, destructive and alienating, Dr. Twenge's conclusions can be helpful to us in understanding the why's and how's of some of the generational issues that we face in the workplace today. We will summarize her research and theses so you understand what the data shows:

Dr. Twenge has researched generational differences by finding data that has been collected throughout time. Unlike a one-time survey, data over time can determine that differences are due to generation or time and not to age. She has conducted these studies using a variation of meta-analysis, finding journal articles and dissertations that gave people psychological scales over a period of several decades in order to track personality changes across generations.

Dr. Twenge used large databases such as Monitoring the Future (high school students) and the American College Freshman Survey (entering college students) for discovering generational differences. Between her own meta-analyses and these two databases, Dr. Twenge's generational studies have drawn from the responses of eleven million young people between the 1930s and the present. These studies have found generational differences in work attitudes, personality traits, attitudes in general, and behaviors. The more research Dr. Twenge did, the more themes of increasing self-focus and individualism began to emerge.

Using the American College Freshman Survey, which has asked nine million young people over the last forty-seven years to rate themselves on self-confidence,; drive to achieve; leadership ability; and public speaking, writing, math, artistic, and academic abilities compared to *their* peers, Dr. Twenge has shown that young people today have an unprecedented level of self-esteem as compared to their 1960–70s counterparts (30% more Millennials than their 60s-70s counterparts scored above the mean). Dr. Twenge also found that the Millennial generation is made of people who are believers of their own greatness without any correlation to actual ability. Twenge also showed that objective test scores actually indicate that writing abilities are far below their 1960s counterparts, despite their own assessment of being above average in writing ability. Twenge further showed that the amount of time spent studying has diminished with little more than a third of the students saying that they study for six or more hours a week compared to almost half of all students claiming the same in the late 1980s. Despite study-ing/working less, her research shows that these young adults' drive to succeed rose sharply. Millennials also have high expectations about getting a graduate degree even though the actual graduate school enrollment is lower than previous generations.[xxviii]

Dr. Twenge identifies elements in pop culture that have influenced the Millennials such as the lyrics to Whitney Houston's "Greatest Love of All"; the popularity of self-admiration phrases such as

"Love yourself," "I am special," and "I love me"; and songs like "I Want To Be a Billionaire" and "The World Should Revolve Around Me." These are just some examples of the "all about me" trend in pop culture that Twenge relies upon to further support her thesis. In her book, *Generation Me*, Twenge identifies culture trends that are impacting the Millennial generation. The belief that there is no longer one right way to do things plays out in a variety of ways among the Millennials: That this generation has not embraced the rules of etiquette that are built around "respect for other people's comfort."[xxix] That cheating in school has increased.[xxx] That students are less likely to recognize the authority of teachers, presuming instead that their perspectives and opinions are on an equal footing with the experts.[xxxi] That former taboos regarding dating and marriage have evaporated.[xxxii] That Millennials are more willing to share their experiences (positive and negative) in explicit detail with anyone who will listen.[xxxiii] And language that was once considered profane has become commonplace.[xxxiv]

A Perfect Storm

These cultural and educational events are working to create what we call "a *perfect storm*." As you may know, a perfect storm is an expression that describes an event "where a rare combination of circumstances will aggravate a situation drastically."[xxxv] Allow us to break it down and describe the perfect storm that has affected Millennials. Our educational system, and society in general, placed a primary emphasis on increasing kids' self-esteem in the years after 1980. We have been in a world where parents praise every child as "special" and, according to Dr. Twenge, "feelings of self-worth are considered a prerequisite to success as opposed to a result of it." Think for a minute how many "All About Me" or similar projects you brought home throughout your preschool, elementary, middle school, and high school education. Max (Harvey's son) and Gabriel and Noah (Mara's sons) have many of these projects that we each have saved. We only now realize how impactful (not necessarily in a good way!) these projects have been in shaping our sons. Self-esteem is not necessarily a bad thing but when, "[it is] based on nothing, [it] does not serve children well in the long run; it's better for children to develop real skills and feel good about accomplishing something," said Martin Seligman, PhD and Master of Applied Positive Psychology.

Nothing exemplifies this better than a recent national headline that read "8-Year-Old Gets 'Catastrophe Award' for Most Homework Excuses." [xxxvi] This is what our education system has come to—rewarding failure. The science is clear, says Ashley Merryman, author (with Po Bronson) of *NurtureShock: New Thinking About Children* and *Top Dog: The Science of Winning and Losing.* "Awards can be powerful motivators, but nonstop recognition does not inspire children to succeed. Instead, it can cause them to underachieve."

Let us give the flip side of this story with an older student. We'll call him George, and he was a senior in high school who was a three-year science research student. George did his research in the nanotechnology lab at Sloan Kettering Cancer Center under the auspices of a noted PhD and his fellows and, together, they created a biochemical fusing of antibodies and radionuclides that greatly improved the efficiency and methodology for detecting cancer. His mentors published a paper and George's name was included among the authors. In his senior year of high school, George was a finalist in his county science competition, which earned him a place in the Intel International Science and Engineering Fair in LA, the most prestigious science competition for high school students throughout the world. He was the first student in the high school's history to earn a spot at Intel. The principal of the school did not make contact with him before he left for the competition in LA and it was two weeks after George returned home with a fourth place overall win before the principal made his way down to the science lab to meet George for the first time. The principal followed up his visit with a letter to George. The first paragraph of the principal's letter is noteworthy and highlights the incongruity of our educational system as the backdrop against the realities of adult life.

> "Dear George: It was a pleasure speaking with you briefly in your science classroom this morning. I want to emphasize my congratulations in a way that I wouldn't be comfortable doing in front of your classmates. We always try to strike a balance between celebrating the accomplishments of individuals, while still supporting and encouraging all. In a letter, however, I can go a little further."

The principal's action, in theory, is positive. But is our country really preparing young people for the real world when we don't publicly single out those who drive distinguished outcomes? We don't take anything away from the principal who acknowledged in his letter that George had accomplished something truly special that the school had rarely seen and that he was impressed by, and proud of, George's accomplishments. But the story causes us to ask why some educators are reluctant to publicly laud distinguished students? Do educators really think that other students will feel diminished in some way? And if they do, perhaps it might spark more competition or motivate another student to be an award-studded science researcher. In our opinion, this highlights a basic failing on some educators' parts to prepare young people for the real world.

Another example of the disparity between our current education system and the real work world is in the area of *praise*. Praise, in education, typically has come in two basic forms: praise for effort and praise for intelligence. Research, under the auspices of psychologist Carol Dweck, PhD, has shown that children perform better if praised for effort. "When we praise children for their intelligence," Dweck says, "we tell them that's the name of the game: look smart, don't risk making mistakes."[xxxvii]

She studied two groups who were given the same challenging task. Both groups performed poorly at the challenging task, but their response to this setback differed greatly. The praised-for-effort group proved to be far more resilient in their attitude toward the challenge. Despite their lack of success and frustration with the task, they proved to be far more willing to try different solutions and give it a go. Dweck further pointed out, "[B]ut the group praised for its intelligence hated the challenging test. They took it as proof they weren't smart."

When these children grow to be young adults and enter the workforce, they are faced with a third kind of praise. Employers are focused on outcomes. You will enter the workplace perhaps with the expectation that you will be praised for being smart or for your effort (showing up and working hard). Employers, though, focus their feedback, performance management programs, and reward systems on outcomes or the process one goes through to get to the outcome (how nicely you "play in the sandbox," how team oriented you are, for example).

Understanding the educational system since the 80s and how it shaped you helps us understand why mentoring, teaching, shaping, and modifying your expectations when you start work are important activities for business leaders to engage in.

Our education system should teach competencies for the real world such as what we find in John Maxwell's book *Failing Forward* and Daniel Pink's book *A Whole New Mind*, which discusses the development of right-brain thinking. Since the system doesn't, it is necessary for you to understand the importance of developing applied skills such as intuition, creativity, empathy, critical and clinical analysis, and resiliency.

Components of a perfect storm have begun to converge: (a) overemphasis on self, (b) parents who overprotect; advocate every argument on behalf of their child; pave the way; shield from failure, harm, and hurt; and do not parent in what child psychologist Madeline Levine calls an authoritative parenting style,[xxxviii] (c) an education system that promotes self-esteem and promotes those who make mistakes or praises the "special" by giving awards and trophies to all equally, and (d) a workforce landscape that is more competitive and demanding of productivity and outcomes than ever and does not treat all men and women equally when it comes to performance reward systems.

So, it is little wonder that young people have high expectations of themselves and others and that their expectations are not being met when they enter the workplace. But what may be shocking to you is that employers characterize young adults as having "outlandish expectations." They experience young adults as the "E" word ... not energetic, not educated, but entitled. While these characterizations may anger you, they shouldn't surprise you.

When the rubber meets the road, two words come to mind: diverging expectations. Employers want young adults to master their jobs and further the organization's and the boss's goals. Let us explore what the research tells us you want.

What the Research Tells Us About What *You* Want From Work

- You want to move up the ladder quickly and get promoted to give you a sense of purpose; you are ambitious and want to lead.
- You want a boss who is a mentor, and you hope that he/she will take you under his/her wing and teach you everything there is to learn.
- You want your time to be respected.
- You don't want to do busy work, you don't want to do a task simply because this is the way it's been done in the

past, and you certainly don't want to feel like you are the lowest person on the totem pole.

- You will do menial tasks in the beginning but once you've done them and have mastered the task, you expect that you will get more substantive work.

- You do not believe in a hierarchy. An organizational chart is merely a way to organize the company. You fundamentally believe that all men and women are created equal at work.

- You want businesses to do more to address society's big challenges, to develop meaningful core values, and to actually be true to those values.

- You want to develop as professionals and, therefore, you want to feel as if you are learning every day.

- You understand that work hours are for purposes of keeping order (from an employer's point of view) but if you need to work from home, that shouldn't be an issue since you're plugged in. If you are going to work for a company, flexibility is key.

- You want to be paid well and receive regular wage increases.

- You believe that once you prove yourself, you will be recognized for your efforts and smarts.

- You want your work environment to be friendly and the people you work with to be upbeat and positive.

- You look for employers who are socially responsible and embrace your desire for challenging work, meaning in the work you do, amazing training and development opportunities, and travel possibilities.[xxxix]

At least one teacher has seen the disconnect between young adults' expectations and the real world and tried to positively influence his students and manage their expectations. High school English teacher David McCullough got national acclaim for his commencement address when he gave graduating seniors at Wellesley High School in Massachusetts some insight into how the real world may view them and tried to manage their expectations. He said:

"You are not special. You are not exceptional. Contrary to what your U9 soccer trophy suggests, your glowing seventh grade report card, despite every assurance of a certain corpulent purple dinosaur, that nice Mister Rogers, and your batty Aunt Sylvia, no matter how often your maternal caped crusader has swooped in to save you … you're nothing special.

Yes, you've been pampered, cosseted, doted upon, helmeted, bubble-wrapped. Yes, capable adults with other things to do have held you, kissed you, fed you, wiped your mouth, wiped your bottom, trained you, taught you, tutored you, coached you, listened to you, counseled you, encouraged you, consoled you and encouraged you again. You've been nudged, cajoled, wheedled and implored. You've been feted and fawned over and called sweetie pie. Yes, you have. And, certainly, we've been to your games, your plays, your recitals, your science fairs. Absolutely, smiles ignite when you walk into a room, and hundreds gasp with delight at your every tweet. Why, maybe you've even had your picture in the Townsman. And now you've conquered high school … and, indisputably, here we all have gathered for you, the pride and joy of this fine community, the first to emerge from that magnificent new building … But do not get the idea you're anything special. Because you're not. If everyone is special then no one is."

McCullough's YouTube videos have received over 2 million hits. His real message though, if you view the YouTube video in total, was about giving back and possessing selflessness but he wanted to get everyone's attention with the "you're not special" message. It was viewed in the press as an overwhelmingly positive, "refreshing" message because the concept of "everyone is special" is not a known practice in the real work world and McCullough wanted to give his high students a "heads up" before they get there.

What the Research Tells *Us* About
How Employers Perceive Young Adults

You are about to enter the working world, a world that is not as nurturing as the world in which you were raised and educated. As we have heard over and again, researchers, educators, and employers feel that young adults are "ill-prepared" and "less able" from a behavioral and emotional intelligence perspective, for that real world. Employers perceive young adults in the following ways:

- You expect a flexible work routine that allows you time for family and personal interests.
- If a job isn't fulfilling and you don't feel as if you are learning every day, you will forsake the job in a minute.

You are believed to have no sense of loyalty to employers.

- You are used to multi-dimensional living and working in a multi-dimensional world and are not willing to feel stifled or have your expectations quashed.
- You have been known to be highly opinionated and fearlessly challenge more experienced people. Status and hierarchy don't impress you much.
- You want to be treated like colleagues rather than subordinates and expect ready access to senior executives, even the CEO, to share your ideas.

Some of these perceptions may seem harsh to you but you're probably saying, "It's true." We have had several young adult clients who were amazed at the number of different and difficult personalities they have found at work and at the dysfunction in the workplace and find themselves at a loss for a strategy in dealing with it.

Take the story of Amy, a 3.9 GPA student at a top university in the country. She landed an internship with a major investment bank. She was also waiting to hear back about an internship at another major investment bank, but when she hadn't heard from them by the time she needed to respond to the first company, she reluctantly accepted the first offer. Five weeks after she started her summer internship there, she called Mara from a street corner, distraught that her boss had been abrupt with her and had told her that a question she had asked was not a smart one. She told Mara that she did not want to work for a company where people treated others so poorly. Mara talked her off the ledge. Mara told her, lovingly, that she would not likely be successful at any company if she wasn't able to constructively handle criticism. After the coaching session,

Amy went back to the office armed with a script that she and Mara had worked on together. Amy asked for a meeting with her boss and expressed to him her thoughts about their not-so-great exchange. She did so in a respectful, honest, and calm way. She told him that she'd felt belittled when he told her that her question was a dumb one, and that she hoped he would appreciate how hard she was working. She agreed that she needed to find answers to questions independent of him (demonstrating self-awareness and accountability) but told him she hoped he would be open to mentoring her. The boss ended up apologizing to her and wrote a note to her. This is what he said:

> "I am very impressed that you feel comfortable giving me upward feedback calmly and so clearly. I've had a lot of [summer associates] in the past and by far you've been the most mature and composed. Always keep true to your convictions even in the bleakest moments. You've been well grounded in sound values and common sense. Thank your parents and family! Again, you rock!"

The boss became her biggest supporter for a full-time position. Amy told me she felt empowered by the experience and resulting feedback from her boss. That's self-esteem based on real-life skills. The big lesson, though, is in the boss's response. He rewarded her for being mature, honest, and able to deal with conflict in a positive way. He didn't blow her off or blackball her. He provided positive reinforcement for positive, mature behavior. Not all bosses are as intuitive and mature as Amy's boss.

Much has been written about young adults today by researchers in order to help educators, businesses, and managers understand how to effectively communicate with and motivate young adults. In this book, we want to help you to acclimate to the culture of your organization. It is important to understand yourself and your expectations and where they may differ from the employer's expectations of you and to use this knowledge to overcome any negative perceptions employers may have about you.[xl]

While you are part of one of the best-educated generations, research shows that you possess attitudes and expectations that could pose challenges once you get into the workplace. The Wall Street Journal recently reported on a study conducted by the Center for Professional Excellence at York College of Pennsylvania. They surveyed 400 human resources professionals about their experience in hiring recent college graduates in a variety of industries and roles. More than a third reported that the level of professionalism among new hires has decreased in the last five years and 45% said that employees' work ethic has worsened. Fifty-two percent of the respondents reported that young employees often appeared arrogant during their interviews or on the job and arrived at the office with an air of entitlement.[xli]

So now you have seen that employers, generally speaking, describe young adults today as:

- Entitled
- Having outlandish expectations
- Wanting to be CEO tomorrow

- Believing that one year of experience makes one an instant expert

A recent survey by CareerBuilder.com showed that the generation's greatest expectations are higher pay (74% of respondents); flexible work schedules (61%); a promotion within a year (56%); and more vacation or personal time (50%).[xlii]

Overcoming Negative Perceptions

So let's learn how to overcome those negative perceptions before you charge out of the workplace gate.

The perception of employers is that:

- Young adults need loads of attention and guidance from employers.
- Young adults like constant positive reinforcement, but don't always take suggestions for improvement well.
- Young people like things spelled out clearly, as they typically flounder without precise guidelines but thrive in structured situations that provide clearly defined rules.

This is not inconsistent with the way young adults have been educated. Education focuses on learning by rubric. A scoring rubric is an attempt to communicate expectations of quality around a task. In many cases, scoring rubrics are used to delineate consistent criteria for grading. Because the criteria are public, a scoring rubric allows teachers and students alike to evaluate criteria, which can be complex and subjective. Students have a clear understanding of the tasks needed to be accomplished in order to get a particular grade.

Do A, B, C, D and E tasks and get an A;

Do A, B, C, D tasks and get a B;

Do A, B, C tasks and get a C and so on.[xliii]

It may seem obvious to you that employees should show up on time, limit lunchtime to an hour, and turn off cell phones during meetings, but those basics aren't necessarily apparent to many young adults today.[xliv] Besides the fact, let's be clear: the real work world does not dole out assignments in a clearly defined and concise way or by using a rubric system.

If you are thinking that the characteristics we discuss in this book don't describe you, please understand one thing. We applaud you for defying the generalizations that the research depicts about young adults today. But did you ever hear the expression that one bad apple spoils the bunch? Well, that is what is happening in the work world. The older generations in the workplace make assumptions about young adults whether you embody the characteristics or not. So you will have to do "double time" to ensure that the powers that be do not lump you in the category of bad apples. It happens so quickly, you won't know what hit you.

Take Olivia, for instance. She had to go to the doctor for a medical condition and asked her boss if it was ok to make up time at the end of the day in order to go to the doctor in the middle of the day. Olivia is very hard working and has established great relationships with other colleagues in her company. Her boss, new to the company, not so much. The boss told her she should take a leave of absence if she has to deal with medical issues. Let's, for a minute, put aside the legal implications of what the boss said and how wrong, on so many levels, it was. The point here is that the boss lumped Olivia together with young people whom she perceives don't have a disciplined work ethic. It was unfair and Olivia had to work really hard to overcome the negative perception that the boss had of her. With a strategy and a script in hand, Olivia met with her boss several times in her attempt to overcome that negative perception. Quite frankly, we are troubled by these negative perceptions. We have met so many young adults who are smart and ambitious and want to make a difference. Part of what motivated us to develop a training program and write our book was to help young adults outsmart the older generations. There are many strategies for young adults to implement that can easily defy these perceptions coming out of the gate.

Let's tackle each one of these negative perceptions, one at a time, in order to help you gain some self-awareness and develop strategies for overcoming these perceptions.

Perception: Spoiled/Entitled[xlv]

Bosses are not going to be like parents who love you no matter what. Part of growing as an employee and professional is learning from past mistakes and accepting constructive criticism. There's no getting out of it. Listen to what your boss has to say . . . talk to him or her about any misperceptions you feel he or she has. Make sure to back up your position with facts (not emotions).[xlvi]

Mara once hired a young woman who was accompanied to work on her first day by her father. People in the office were aghast. Her father told us he wanted to see where she was going to work and to meet the people with whom she was going to work. If your parent doesn't have the instinct to know better, you must. Do not have your parent accompany you to work. Call your boss or the HR department to inquire about anything relating to your employment. It is simply a BCM (bad career move) to have your parent do this for you. From the employer's perspective, it will look like you are relying on your parents to pave the way, protect you, and shield you from adversity. They may worry that if there are any decisions to be made, your parents' input and guidance will have a front row seat.

Perception: Lazy

Working hard, harder than anyone else, is the number one item on the work to-do list. That may mean coming in early, staying late, and working some weekends. In today's world, you can work almost anywhere so when we say work weekends, it may mean answering emails or drafting a report, which can be done pretty much from anywhere.

There really isn't room for lazy and disinterested people in the business world. It's just moving too fast and there often are not enough hours in the day. Think about how you wish to perform the job you have been asked to do. Colleagues and bosses are not going to give you the rubric (how-to guide) spelling out exactly how you are to do the job. You want the reputation as a high-energy and high-level-thinking worker.

Perception: Poor Work Ethic

You may need to alter your perceptions about work, especially for entry-level positions in which workers have historically been expected to put the time in to earn their due. You may feel that you already know this, but your boss may not agree. Take this scenario for a moment. You are working for six months for a big company in the finance department and your best friend's brother is getting married. You need to take off three days for the destination wedding and festivities. If you merely ask for three days off for the wedding, your boss could immediately form the perception (albeit not a correct one) that "Here we go again—another one who doesn't know what hard work is." You will have to actively prevent this perception from surfacing. First, you could start the conversation with your boss by saying something like this:

> "I have a wedding of a close friend in Las Vegas, and I am requesting a few days off four months

from now. I know that this may not be the ideal time, but I am committed to meeting all my deadlines. I will be in full communication with the office except for my traveling time and the actual wedding ceremony. If we have a huge project going on at the time, I will leave the day before the wedding and fly out the next morning. If I can take the full three days off, given the workload, I ask permission to do so. I will even take the time without pay, if that is required."

Our prediction is that your boss will be much more amenable to you taking the time with that approach than if you simply ask for three days off for your best friend's brother's wedding.

Perception: Lacking Respect for Authority

Choose battles carefully and don't question every single decision made. Sometimes you will see the end point faster than other people (even those more senior to you) will see them. Sometimes you will think you know the direction in which to proceed while others more senior to you seem unable to make a decision or can't see the end point.

You, as an entry-level or first-few-years-out worker, have to pick and choose when you want to convey your opinion or question the path your boss is treading. Remember, your boss is the "captain" for a reason and may possibly be thinking of things that you aren't aware of, like the deep political landscape of the organization.

Your boss may be thinking about how best to negotiate what he or she wants to accomplish given his own challenging relationship with his boss. Your boss may want to be methodical about the process the team travels to get to the end point. It is not your role to rush that process. Sometimes in business, it's the process that is most important to getting to the end result.

You will look and sound smart if you ask questions that lead your boss down the decision-making path or cause him to think about something he may not have thought about. When asking questions, be sure only to ask the question that you can't possibly find the answer to anywhere else. You don't want to be the gnat that buzzes around your boss's head constantly asking questions and causing him to want to swat at you. Also, save all the questions for one round so you avoid going back several times. You will appear to be efficient and courteous of your boss's time.

Perception: Too Focused on Teamwork and Not Focused Enough on Your Individual Role

Almost all work will be some blend of individual assignments and teamwork with people of different ages and with diverse backgrounds. You need to know when to play your individual position and when to be part of a team. You were hired to do your job, and you must know when you need to perform on your own.

Mara had an assistant to whom she gave an assignment of writing a letter. The assistant knew the purpose of the letter and to whom it was going. She clearly understood the information that needed to be conveyed as that was discussed in a prior meeting. A half hour later the assistant came into Mara's office and asked, "What do you want me to say in the letter?" The assistant had failed in playing her individual position. Mara had asked her to write the letter and needed her to think about what it needed to say based on their extensive conversation regarding the purpose of the letter. In other words, Mara had given her the answers when they spoke about the content. Mara told her assistant that she needed her to think of the words and write a draft based on what they had discussed. The assistant said that she thought they could write it together. Bad answer.

Perception: Unrealistic Expectations

Pace yourself and gain the requisite experience and skills before expecting recognition in the form of a promotion. This will be the most challenging of perceptions to overcome. We all have expectations that go unfulfilled and cause us to be disappointed and unhappy.

The work pace is much slower than what the information age has presented to each of us. The culture of some organizations may not embrace change and processing of new ideas as easily and quickly as you would expect.

While some big organizations are modifying their approach to performance management to better understand the expectations of young adults, there is no substitute for skills building. The worst thing that can happen to you is being moved into a position that is above your skill level. It could be a recipe for disaster.

Companies develop core competencies for each job level. These are the requirements that one needs to meet to be able to master the job level at hand. You won't be qualified to advance to the next level until you are able to master all of those requirements.

But mastering all of the requirements doesn't necessarily result in a job promotion. There are many factors that go into the decision to promote someone. Some of those factors may have nothing to do with whether you are qualified; cost, business need, and the competition all are factors that are not within your control.

Perception: Not Committed to Work

Conduct research on prospective employers to find organizations that have career paths, core values, and a mission that are meaningful to you. In the end, work is work and you may not be presented with a new learning experience every day. In the beginning, your career should be about building skills, expertise, and experience and you need to show that you are committed to the work even when it is not exciting.

As an attorney, Mara has drafted thousands of termination letters and negotiated an equal number of termination packages. One could argue that doing the same thing over and over again is boring. It very well could be. But here is the thing. You only get really good at something if you do it over and over again—the proverbial practice makes perfect. You see, it is a cycle that helps you create expertise. You do something repeatedly, you refine your technique over time, you get recognized for your work and expertise, you begin to feel good about your work and your expertise, and you then begin to develop passion[xlvii] for what you do. Our theory on passion is that you really can't experience passion until you become really good at something, you experience success at doing it, others seek you out because you are successful at it, and you can turn it into a way to make a living. Passion follows skill and success. By the way, while Mara has done thousands of termination letters and negotiations for separation packages, each one is slightly different, giving her the necessary variety in the routine nature of drafting the same type of legal document. Just when you think that the work you are assigned is getting boring, ask yourself if you are mastering a skill that is valuable and whether you are gaining an expertise in something by doing it repetitively. Ask yourself whether you are sought out by others because you do the particular task well. If the answer to these questions is yes, you will have opportunities to seek advancement, change jobs and become further credentialed in your field. If the answer to these questions is no, your goal should be to become engaged and more committed in the work you are doing in order to gain the requisite experience and expertise needed today.

Perception: No Loyalty to Employers

Try not to doubt the motives of employers and learn to trust them while continuing your professional development. This is not an easy thing to do. But understand this—it is very expensive to lose employees. Companies call this the cost of turnover, the churn rate at which an employee enters and leaves an organization in a given year. It is an important human resources metric that causes employers to focus on retaining their current workforce and on planning for the future. Whether it seems that way or not, your employer has a vested interest in keeping its employees generally happy and engaged. This is particularly the case with respect to employers and their young adult employees. Companies, generally speaking, continue to find ways to make the workplace an environment where young adults want to be.

Turnover is broken down into *voluntary turnover* (the company did not take the initiative in terminating the employment of an individual; the individual made the decision to leave the company, got a new job, or decided to leave on his own) and *involuntary turnover* (the company made the decision to terminate the employment of the individual or individuals as a result of a layoff, poor performance, or bad acts on the part of the employee).

The list of potential indirect costs of employee turnover includes:

- Lost productivity associated with the interim period before a replacement can fill the job, the time a coworker spends away from his or her work to help fill the gap, and low employee morale.
- The cost of formal and informal training to get the new employee up to speed.
- Severance pay or litigation costs from involuntary turnovers.
- Costs for advertising and promotional materials, referral bonuses, relocation expenses.

The average worker today stays at each of his or her jobs for 4.4 years, according to the most recent available data from the Bureau of Labor Statistics, but the expected tenure of the workforce's youngest employees is about half that.

Ninety-one percent of Millennials expect to stay in a job for less than three years, according to the Future Workplace *Multiple Generations @ Work* survey of 1,189 employees and 150 managers.[xlviii] That means they would have fifteen to twenty jobs over the course of their working lives! So stop and think about whether you can have a longer-term career at your company. Obviously, if there is no growth, you should seek other opportunities. Employers, though, are on the lookout for job hoppers and are most reluctant to hire them because of the high cost of turnover.[xlix]

Perception: Lacking in Social Skills

In order to reduce the expectations gap, young adults need to use communications and diversity skills differently in the workplace. It is a skill to be able to socialize and communicate with people of diverse backgrounds. Having more face-to-face engagements and enhancing your oral and written communications will be the biggest challenge of any young adult today in the workplace.

It will be incumbent upon you to pick yourself up and walk down the hall or take the elevator a floor or two to see the person with whom you are having a deep e-conversation. You will distinguish yourself by doing this because the instinct today is to continue pecking away at the keyboard. Daniel Pink, in his book *A Whole New Mind*, calls this "high concept, high touch." This is what Daniel Pink has to say about this.

> "We are moving from an economy and society built on the logical, linear, computer-like capabilities of the Information Age to an economy and a society built on the inventive, empathic, big-picture capa-

bilities of what's rising in its place, the Conceptual Age. High concept involves the capacity to detect patterns and opportunities, to create artistic and emotional beauty, to craft a satisfying narrative, and to combine seemingly unrelated ideas into something new. High touch involves the ability to empathize with others, to understand the subtleties of human interaction, to find joy in one's self and to elicit it in others, and to stretch beyond the quotidian in pursuit of purpose and meaning."[1]

As a society, we need to get back to basics—building relationships that are substantive, meaningful, and purposeful. We can't do that by sitting at our desks and avoiding human interaction.

Perception: In Need of Much Oversight and Direction

The way to overcome this negative perception is to do everything you can to run with it. That's right. Run with everything you are given. Go beyond the "four corners" of the job description by working independently and with little direction. There's a catch. You cannot go radio silent. You need to communicate with your coworkers and boss what you are doing and how you are doing it. It is important to check in to make sure you are on the right path with your job duties or project but remember that your job is not a group project.

There is always something to think about and do that doesn't fall squarely on the list of duties you are required to do. Do that, too.

Yes, go beyond the job by thinking of something that no one asked you to do or think about. Let your boss know you thought about that or you did the extra task. You will be looked upon as someone who goes beyond the call of duty. That is a good thing and will certainly distinguish you from others who merely do what they are told.[li]

Chapter 3

Sailing in Calm Waters and Building Legitimate Self-Esteem

Your Strengths, Weaknesses, and Social Style – Your Compass

What makes you the way you are? What are the differences between you and others?

In your preparation for job applications and interviews, you will have learned a lot about yourself, your characteristics, your way of working, and your preferences for all types of work. Some of this will have become apparent during your school years, but what people like and dislike changes, and their ways of doing things become refined. You may have discovered things you are interested in, even passionate about.

Now suppose you had a teenage interest in computer gaming, basketball, model making, whatever. This is not necessarily going to be part of your working life. But the general principle may be. That means you need to think about the essence of what that interest is. What is the key piece such that, if it wasn't there, you wouldn't be inspired to engage in that pastime? For example, you are a whiz at computer games. Which ones in particular, and what are the challenges they present to you? How do you go about meeting those challenges? What value does this activity represent? Could it be precision or elegance or determination? All kinds of things reflect upon the way you go about doing things.

Often, the thing that you do is hidden from you because you think it's ordinary—everyone does that, don't they? The thing is, they probably don't. Try this: ask your friends what they think you do that is special, something they don't do, something they would come to you for advice, your expertise, your know-how.

A piece of advice on this: your expertise may well change over time. As you gain more experience in a variety of settings, your specialty is likely to get refined, or even change as you realize that "well, actually, that is subsumed under X."

So check in with yourself, from time to time … for the rest of your life! What is the essence of what you do, the way you go about in the world? It's going to be something fairly general, applicable in lots of different ways: "I bring order to chaos," "I make things easier to do," "I provide a sense of calm," or "I light up a room." And when you have had a number of jobs, think back to what you ended up doing in them, or wanted to do but couldn't (which is why you left).

Now in your school days you will have, no doubt, discovered things you really hate doing. Write a brief list of them and then eliminate any that were primarily based on the personality of the teacher or mannerisms of the person who was in charge of this activity. Then look at your list and work out what it was about those activities that turned you off. There's a good probability that these things will be present in the working environment, so you need to know what to do if you encounter them. One of the main reasons people give up on things is because they think, "I don't see the point," "I don't know why I'm doing this," "What good is it?" and so on. In the work world, you may not see the point or value in what you are asked to do. Many times, your boss or manager will not explain the point. They just expect you to do the task; the very task you hate doing. When you encounter this, attempt to have a conversation with your manager or boss about how the task fits into the larger project. It is possible that the conversation may lead to a different way of doing the task or, through the discussion, the boss may expand the task into something more meaningful or he may even see that it is not as important as he had originally believed it to be.

It is true that when you understand the reason for doing something, you will be far more motivated to do it. So, if you are in a work situation, you need to clarify for yourself (and for others) what the intended outcome is. Your boss or team leader has probably already worked this out (they usually have) but they need to tell you as well so that you understand it in your terms. That could mean getting a clearer picture of the whole process the organization is engaged in, whether it's assembling mobile phone apps or organizing seminars for international conferences. You should find out how the piece you're involved in fits in with the big picture so that you can see how you are contributing, and who, down the line, depends on your efforts to be able to complete their job.

Finding Your Heading

During the interview process and beyond, you will be called upon to establish your goals and objectives and determine how they fit with corporate goals and objectives. Success does not come easy. Sometimes, you'll find yourself on the tough career road. While it may not feel so when you are there, it is the better road to take. People going into the work world with a more realistic mindset, ready for setbacks and expecting to spend the time necessary to be successful, will be better off in the end. As an added bonus, any social psychologist will tell you that the more effort and sacrifice people make toward something, the more committed they will be to it. Indeed, as we watch successful innovators—ranging from the teams taught at Stanford's design school to the people responsible for the amazing journey of the famous animation company, Pixar—the most successful tend to have this "it is going to be tough, but I can and will do it" mindset. We have seen many young people who want to bail when the going gets tough. It is our strong belief and experience that the tough times are what make us better professionals. Those tough experiences help shape our business outlooks and judgment and help us develop our own styles of leadership. Here are some tips when it comes to outcomes.

In a discussion about his character Tom Avery in the film *The Way* (2011), Martin Sheen says that Tom's journey was more important than the goal. Indeed, when the character arrived in Compostela, he immediately wondered, "Now what?"

We need goals, outcomes, to motivate us into action. Alfred Hitchcock called the thing sought after a McGuffin—a vague something that motivates the character to act, to engage with the world, to create some change. But obtaining the McGuffin, achieving the goal, is not what matters. What's more important is how you respond, the action you take—what you do when you are faced with a novel situation.

Every small change you make has some unpredictable knock-on effects. That's why you need to *expect the unexpected* and *expect to fail* (or at the least, have setbacks) because it is by failing or having setbacks that we learn. It's how we improve our understanding of the world, how we adjust and correct what we do to improve the chances of getting what we want. Well, that's our rationale. We like to think we can get better at doing things, but we still have to contend with an uncertain universe and unanticipated events.

So what is the point of having a well-formed outcome? (In the business world, they often refer to SMART outcomes.) Is it useful? Sure it is. Especially when you are working with things in the world, it's better to be specific in order to get things done on time, on schedule, and on budget. But in life in general? It's a McGuffin that gets you moving, but it's not the main thing. Your stated outcome acts like a compass, keeping you focused and on track whenever you stray from the path.

20 Things About Outcomes

1. Given a choice, shun the "easy option" and go for the path less traveled, the challenge, because that way you will learn more.

2.   Have a can-do mindset.

3.   The journey is usually more important than the goal.

4.   Achieving an outcome often creates a void in which you have to ask, "What next?"

5.   What matters is how you conducted yourself along the way.

6.   We want surprises. (We only want exactly what we specified if we're in manufacturing.)

7.   Expect the unexpected. Expect to fail or experience setbacks.

8.   Adopt a positive glass-half-full mindset. Think about "What went well today?"

9.   Have "strong opinions, weakly held." (Paul Saffo).

10.   Sutton's Law: "If you think that you have a new idea, you are wrong. Someone else probably already had it. This idea isn't original either; we stole it from someone else."

11.   Hofstadter's Law: It always takes longer than you expect, even if you take Hofstadter's Law into account.

12.   The value in SMART outcome setting? What really matters is that now it makes sense to act, to take the first step, and notice what happens, and if necessary, make adjustments.

13.   Carry out a *pre-mortem* (Gary Klein). A pre-mortem is a managerial strategy in which a manager imagines that a project or organization has failed and then works backward to determine what potentially could lead to the failure of the project or organization. The technique breaks possible group thinking by facilitating a positive discussion on

threats, increasing the likelihood the main threats are identified. Management can then analyze the magnitude and likelihood of each threat and take preventative actions to protect the project or organization from suffering an untimely death.[lii]

14. Does the particular outcome mesh with the company's/organization's overarching aims?

15. One of the main benefits of thinking about outcomes is that you have to think about the future, and how do we get there from here? There are two solutions: (a) somebody has already done this. Find out and follow their path—and tweak it. (b) It's new, there is no path to follow, you have to create your own path—explore and learn.

16. Don't start until you can envision going through the whole process.

17. Having a structure (usually) makes it easy and saves you mental effort. But it may limit your options/understanding because you're not engaged in the process in the same way.

18. We want more than we asked for: added value, some bonus features (but we can't pre-plan them).

19. Plan your outcome to cover a range of people's needs: What do *they* want?

20. Taking action invites risk; how much depends partly on you. How willing are you to leave your comfort zone?

Getting Up Steam

For your desire to be motivating, it's not enough to imagine you already have it. Research has shown that merely dreaming about your desired outcome—the penthouse suite, the flashy sports car, the successful entrepreneurship—actually demotivates you because your brain can't distinguish that well between reality and imagination and thinks you've already got it. So you relax, your enthusiasm drops, and you do nothing—your desire has "melted into thin air."

What you need to do instead, according to psychologist Gabriele Oettingen (Oettingen 2014), is to add some steps to the process. First, you have the dream. That's important, and you think positively about what that will get you—the evidence, if you like, of having achieved that dream. Then comes a vital step that she calls Mental Contrasting. What obstacles are in your way? Not external things, but those personal traits that you know will get in your way—your laziness, your untidiness, your need to chill out, your need to get online rather than meet face-to-face. Take a bit of time thinking your way through these downers.

Finally, you need to plan how you will deal with those things when they crop up, because they surely will. Have a plan in the form of "If [situation X] arises, then I need to do [behavior Y]." This has to be some kind of "goal-directed behavior." You are practicing a kind of "mental rehearsal technique." You know from your experience that you're very likely to sabotage yourself, so in order to get out of your own way, you set up your strategy ahead of time. Then, when the opportunity for sabotage occurs—as it will—your unconscious mind recognizes this and knows what to do.

A particular goal is merely a milestone. Once you've achieved it, stop and think about the bigger reality. "What was that outcome part of? How does it fit into the bigger picture of my life?" Essentially, you have to answer the question, "What next? What do I do now that I've achieved that goal?"

Therefore, having just one goal is not enough. Think "Sequel," think "Series." You need goals on a number of levels and with different time spans, even up to and including the end of your life. But steady on, you haven't left the dock yet, and you have no idea what could happen once you set sail, so let's get thinking about the opening stages of your working life first—and that has a number of definable steps.

Marker Buoys

How do you know you're heading in the right direction? You've headed out into the unchartered seas intent on completing the list of goals and objectives you created earlier. All good things. But, starting out on what you think is the correct heading does not assure your success. You should expect that your path will be altered along the way. The swells of change and the cross-currents of unexpected challenges can toss you hither and yon to the point where you're not sure you're still on the right path or even if your compass is still working. You need to continually monitor your bearings.

That's where marker buoys come in. They are essentially process checkpoints. When heading into any port, the marker buoys indicate your safe passage home. They mark where the trouble spots lie; where the deep water is; where the objects are just under the surface that you need to avoid so you don't become shipwrecked. They're guideposts. You've seen them before—maybe in movies—those bobbing orange and white floating mini-islands that rock from side to side, perhaps with a bell on the top that clangs in the fog. They let you know where the safe routes are as you travel from one place to another.

Once you chart your goals/objectives, but before you set sail, you need to create your own marker buoys to help you stay on course. For each goal you create, you need to create a series of process checkpoints along the way. This is where you set your expectations. At marker buoy "A," I expect to have accomplished this or that. At marker buoy "B," I expect to have achieved thus and so. They act as mini-goals that you use to make sure that you are where you want/need to be in order to stay on your predetermined course. When you reach marker buoy "A," you assess where you're at. Are you on track and exactly where you want/need to be? If not, what has thrown you off course? What needs to be done to get you back on course? Or even more important, based on the events that have taken you off course, do you need to change your ultimate goal … change course … because you now have more data to use to set a different course in your life.

The point is, sailors often set sail with a predetermined course … with marker buoys to help assess progress toward goals. Just be open to the fact that the blowing winds of change and the strong currents of events may require you to be flexible to the need to modify (and monitor) your course. You may need to redo your charts as your life unfolds.

Chapter 4

Clear Sailing: 20 Ways
to Distinguish Yourself

We have come up with twenty ways to distinguish yourself in the workplace that we teach in our training program, "Sharpen-UrEdge"™. They may seem simple or even old-fashioned. But trust us, they are tips that will set you apart from others. Business is based on traditions that have been around for a long time and is made up of people who prefer to do business with people they like and whose relationships they have cultivated.

Tip #1. Online vs. Face-to-Face Communications (The Walk Down the Hall)

> "It's hard to say exactly what it is about face-to-face contact that makes deals happen, but whatever it is, it hasn't yet been duplicated by technology."
>
> *Paul Graham*

We do this exercise with young adults in our workshops. We get everyone out of their seats and have them follow us down the hall. We are on a mission and no one is quite sure what that mission is but we all follow the leader down the hall. Inevitably, we find an office, we knock, peek our heads into the office, say hello and do an about face back down the hall to the workshop room. Everyone sits down. Ok then. "What was that about?" Mara asks. There is always one in the crowd that yells out, "Seventh inning stretch?"

It was the walk down the hall. You will never forget the walk down the hall. Why is that important? It's important because we all are deep in conversation online with our colleagues all day long. We type and type and type away. We can have a detailed discussion, a debate, or even a fight on a subject online. Forget the fact that we are creating a paper trail that can sometimes be very problematic if a conflict ever blows up and results in a lawsuit. Many times so much is lost in translation with online conversations and discussions. Things can be misinterpreted. Emotions can be read into statements where such emotions were not intended to be conveyed.

Our advice is to get up out of your seat, get away from your keyboard, and go meet face-to-face with the person with whom you are deep in discussion. It will make a difference in your relationship, in the conversation, and in what you are working on together.

The walk down the hall can be very meaningful.

Tip #2. The Value of the Telephone – Respect for Receptivity

"The most compelling reason for most people to buy a computer for the home will be to link it to a nationwide communications network. We're just in the beginning stages of what will be a truly remarkable breakthrough for most people—as remarkable as the telephone."

Steve Jobs

As with the walk down the hall, the telephone is your friend! It is pretty comical how young adults shun the telephone. Avoiding the phone in favor of emailing is hurting business.[liii] There is no room for phone aversion in business when a lot of business is premised on client–service provider or consumer–customer service relationships and on personal rapport. When you have to give bad news or a difficult message, always do so in person or by telephone, if in person is not feasible. Many young adults are faced with turning down job offers. We actually hired an intern once who never informed us that she wasn't going to come work for us. She just never followed up after her semester ended. Really bad form.

Showing interest and being approachable and open are qualities that are respected in the workplace. It is easy for someone to ignore an email. While someone can also avoid taking your call, it is so much less common for young adults to make phone calls that when they do, people may be more apt to respond.

This reminds us of a story. Mara had a client's dad call her and tell her that his son was leaving his public school to go to private school. He was doing this for both a new academic challenge and for basketball, his passion. The father asked Mara if it was ok for his son to write to his current high school coach and let him know in an email that his son was leaving the team and public school to go to private school.

The relationship with the coach was strained, which was one of the reasons his son had decided to leave the school. Mara told the father unequivocally, "No, it's not all right for your son to write an email. Your son must call the coach to arrange a face-to-face meeting." Mara said she would script the conversation for him but he must talk to him in person. The father told Mara his son was not up for that and wouldn't do it. Mara asked him why he had called her.

In the course of the conversation, he asked Mara three times whether his son could have this conversation in an email. Mara said no each time. Mara then sent him a script on what his son should say and called him to practice the conversation. His son mustered the power to arrange a meeting with the coach and he told the coach in person that he was leaving to go to private school. The coach wished him well and commended him for coming in to talk to him in person. The coach told him that it took a lot of courage to come in to meet with him, and that he knew the client would be successful as a student athlete wherever he went. The client felt validated.

Another story. We do this exercise in our workshop to practice talking on the telephone. We ask for a volunteer and always get an eager young man (funny how it's always a young man)! We pull out of our bag of tricks a Fisher Price phone, which everyone thinks is ridiculously elementary. And right they are. It is elementary but we are teaching an elementary skill—talking on the telephone.

The young man inevitably looks unnerved. We tell the group and the young man that Mara is the CEO of Company X, and he has gotten an offer to join her company for his first job. We then say that Company Y has also offered him a job and he likes that job much better than the job at Mara's company. We instruct the young man to call Mara on the telephone and tell her that he is not going to accept Mara's offer.

The young men who volunteer for this exercise inevitably are stumped. They don't know where to start. This happens every time we do the exercise. The audience is getting more and more uncomfortable watching their peers stumble over their words. One voice from the group, in an obvious cry to end the humiliation, yells, "Hang up the phone!!!" Then something magical happens. The volunteer's peers start yelling out all the things he should say:

> "Thank you so much for the time you and your colleagues spent with me during my many interviews. I really liked everyone with whom I spoke and the environment at Company X is really energized. I have thought long and hard about this opportunity. I wanted to let you know that I have been offered an opportunity at another company and after much deliberation, I have decided to accept their offer. There were many factors that went into my decision but one thing is for sure—the decision was difficult. I would like to be able to keep the lines of communication open in case I wish to make

a job change in the future. Again, thank you for all of your time and kindness throughout the interview process."

Remember these words: *Pick Up the Phone* ...

Tip #3. We vs. I

"Coming together is a beginning; keeping together is progress; working together is success."

Henry Ford

Have you ever tuned into the radio station WIIFM? Ok, it was a trick question. The call letters stand for "What's In It For Me?" There is nothing worse that you can do coming out of the gate and into the workplace than to tune into WIIFM.

The natural instinct is to ask yourself "What's in it for me?" But working for others requires more. This is about finding what is in it for them. Why do they carry out their business in the way they do? What drives the company? It may not be what you thought at first. Once you're in a job, you begin to find out what actually motivates others—it's what they focus on, pay attention to, and prioritize. The thought that needs to consume you during your first years in the workplace is "What can I do for others?" This will come back to you in a very positive way because you will be known for helping others be successful. Companies want to know that you are there to help achieve the company's goals. Your boss will be pleased if you are constantly thinking of ways to make the boss or your department/team look good.

Tip #4. All-Hands-On-Deck
(Organizational Savvy/Socio-Political Matrix)

> "Leadership is not about a title or a designation. It's about impact, influence and inspiration. Impact involves getting results, influence is about spreading the passion you have for your work, and you have to inspire teammates and customers."
>
> *Robin Sharma*

Organizational Savvy: The Socio-Political Matrix

Joel DeLuca was a consultant, a prolific writer, and the author of the book *Political Savvy*. During his years as a proponent of organizational savvy (or know-how), he developed a method of targeting those few key individuals inside the organization that you would want to influence in order to spread your own influence throughout the company. It was a way of efficiently using one's own influence to impact a much broader audience. We've used this methodology successfully for years to become more effective leaders and to maneuver through the rough waters of organizational politics. For young adults, combining this targeting tool with the knowledge gained from becoming more versatile will make you a much more effective/positive worker and leader … one who others willingly want to follow.

How the Socio-Political Matrix works

The purpose of the socio-political matrix is to assist you in determining who in your organization you should target for your influence. That person should be someone who is powerful enough politically to make a difference, is connected to the most people, and is the most in favor of your issue or proposal. In the example below, you can see how a small matrix lays out. You vastly expand your leadership influence by gaining the support and advocacy of more politically powerful allies who can carry your issues and ideas forward to others of influence in your organization on your behalf.

Issue to resolve (example): You need funding for your team's project
Not in favor of your issue   *In favor of your issue*

Step 1: List out your issue. For example, you need funding for your team's project

Step 2: List out the leaders in your organization who you believe may have an impact on whether your issue can be resolved in your favor. Rank them by power (the most powerful at the top).

Step 3: Take a guess as to what degree each leader is either for or against your issue. In the above example, Leader A is mildly against your issue while Leader E absolutely loves your issue.

Step 4: Draw lines of connection between the "Xs" based on who you think/know are strongly connected to each other; they may report to each other or have worked together in the past. You can see in the above example that Leader C is not really connected to the most powerful leader (Leader A).

Step 5: Your target of influence (using your versatility) will be the leader who is the most powerful, who is connected to the most people, who loves your issue and is malleable (able to be influenced by you if necessary).

What you do is convince that person to be an advocate for your issue. Using his/her connections and affiliations for your issue, they may be able to influence the others (especially the most powerful leader) to change their minds in your favor. Since leaders D and E are in favor of your issue, you can also enlist their help in influencing the decisions of leader A. The socio-political matrix is a great tool for young adults because you tend to be collaborative. Looking for connections in all the right places is nothing new to you.

To distill this theory, there are three words you have to remember when you think about the socio-political matrix and possessing organizational savvy:

- Who has the *power* to make a decision
- Who may or may not have *power* but is *malleable* enough to be in favor of your position or issue (in other words, who is able to be easily influenced, make a difference), and
- Who is *connected* to the most people.

In the mid-part of Mara's career, she demonstrated organizational savvy without even knowing it and worked the socio-political matrix at her international law firm. She had drafted an employment policy that was very much needed. After doing so, she had to influence the powers that be to adopt the policy.

Walking into an all-male management committee meeting to promote a parental leave policy when she was eight months pregnant wasn't exactly a GPM (Good Professional Move!). She decided to enlist a female partner, Maureen Brundage, who was really well liked and respected but did not, at that time, have a huge amount of power within the firm. Power was clearly defined then as who "sat at the executive table" and who brought in the most amount of revenue.

Maureen was glad to take Mara's proposal (the cost analysis, the actual proposed policy, and the business case) to a few (male) members on the management committee. Maureen chose to speak with one partner with whom she had a close relationship and whom she knew could help influence some of the other members. Maureen told them that if they have any questions, they should call Mara. Mara methodically chose a person who was completely in favor of her proposal but who didn't have enough clout or power to approve the policy outright. That person, in turn, spoke to someone with more power who had to be convinced that this was a good idea. He, in turn, spoke to the Chairman of the Management Committee, who didn't quite favor this kind of policy but was malleable given the right business case arguments.

Eventually, the Chairman called Mara and she passionately made her best arguments! It did not cost her her job and the next day, the firm adopted the policy. Mara naturally used the political and social power and influence structure of the firm to get this very important policy passed.

Tip #5. First Impressions Go a Long Way (90-Day Rule/Listen)

"We don't know where our first impressions come from or precisely what they mean, so we don't always appreciate their fragility."

Malcolm Gladwell

Everyone who starts a new job, whether an entry-level worker or an experienced hire, has a basic instinct to prove themselves coming out of the gate. We advise clients who are starting a new job, regardless of their level, that there is a 90-day rule.[liv] For the first 90 days, do what is assigned and go on a listening tour. Make time to speak, even informally, with everyone you can, both those within your department and those outside who interact with your department. Ask them questions about their job. Ask them what works for them and doesn't work for them. Let them know that you are curious about how the organization operates and the best way for you to do that is to meet as many people as you can and find out what they do and what makes them tick. People love talking about themselves and their lives (work lives, of course!). You will be viewed as a person who cares about others, is inquisitive and isn't out to prove how great you are.

Tip #6. Take the Time to Understand the Culture

"No company, small or large, can win over the long run without energized employees who believe in the mission and understand how to achieve it."

Jack Welch

It is important that you understand the "personal" culture of the organization for whom you work. Does your workplace feel and act like a family? Is it an entrepreneurial or risk-taking culture? Is it a competitive and achievement-oriented culture or is it a highly structured, hierarchal culture? Is your workplace a passive-aggressive culture (the category takes its name from the organization's quiet but tenacious resistance, in every way but openly, to corporate directives)?[lv] Is your organization innovative, competitive, aggressive, performance outcome driven, team oriented, detail oriented, socially responsible and/or fast or slow to make decisions? It is important you understand the personal culture so that you can adapt if you need to in order to fit into the organization and not go against the tide.

HR Professional Tom Armour calls cultural fit the "single most important element when hiring people. Skills and experience are very important, but if a person does not fit with the company's culture they will either leave or be terminated, usually in a matter of months," says Armour, who also is cofounder of High Return Selection, a firm that helps companies recruit top-level talent. "We often remind companies: Is this a person who you will enjoy having on the team for the next five years?"

Armour says good cultural fit is a prerequisite for whether a candidate will move forward in the interview process. Specific skills, he said, can be taught, while cultural fit cannot.

14 Ways to Determine the Culture

- Ask to interview an employee or two on what they enjoy about working there.
- Ask for a walk-through of the office—listen for laughs and look for smiles; that says a lot about the work environment. (Do the employees personalize their workspace? Pictures or quotations on the wall?)
- Ask about previous people who held the position if you are replacing someone. Find out what they did right and what they could've done better.
- Look at sites like Glassdoor.com for reviews by current or former employees.
- Keep in mind that there are "pockets" of culture within individual departments, so the overall company culture could differ from your specific work area. That's why it's important to try to do things like bullets 1 and 2 above.
- Ask what sorts of behavior are rewarded and which are punished.
- Ask how (or if) news that affects the company is shared. Does everyone learn of it at once or is it distributed to managers to trickle down to employees? Are they transparent?
- Find out what sort of events the company holds for employees. Is it a once-a-year Christmas party or are there monthly opportunities to celebrate with coworkers?
- Ask if there are known slackers in the office and try to find

out why they are still around (good luck with this one, but if you get a straight answer, you will have a leg up).

- Ask about how difficult it is to get attention or funding for new ideas and initiatives —are they a "we've always done it that way" type of company?
- Ask what the company's overall mission/vision is. If a random employee can tell you (at least in general terms) it could signify a strong, unified, and well-informed workforce.
- Ask about the dress code and other abrasive policies/details that, while palatable at first, can end up chafing you down the line.
- Find out if the company offers any sort of reimbursement or support for training, seminars, or graduate school tuition. If they value smart employees who work to better themselves, they probably will.
- Ask how previous employees who committed ethics violations were held accountable. (General terms are fine to protect any guilty parties, but do they even care about ethics in the first place?)

Tip #7. Mr. Taylor – Respect The Authority Figure

"We don't need to share the same opinions as others, but we need to be respectful."

Taylor Swift

You are probably wondering why we call this tip "Mr. Taylor." The reference was created by Mara's close friends, Betsy, a lawyer by education and training and now a short movie producer and editor for the nonprofit world, and her husband, Ted, the former CEO of his family's mid-market financial services business. We say former because, several years ago, Ted and his brother sold their family business to a large financial services company.

Betsy always envied Ted for not having "a boss" to whom to report. In the early part of her career, Betsy would come home day after day and tell Ted the tales of Mr. Taylor, her boss, the least of which was that he made his subordinates call him Mr. Taylor.

Betty recounts the terror and frustration she lived with every day of her early career, worrying about what arbitrary demand Mr. Taylor would make on her and her team. The day after Ted sold the family business, he reported to work, as the business deal stated that he and his brother would continue to lead the business on behalf of the buyer. When Betsy greeted him at the front door after Ted returned from work that first day after the sale of the business, she asked him, "So, how's Mr. Taylor?" A stark realization to them both was that Ted now had a boss.

Mr. Taylor represents all bosses, good and bad. Always remember that your boss is a boss for a reason. Someone higher on the corporate ladder believes he or she is worthy of the title "boss." Until that higher order doesn't think so, it is not your job to question the boss's authority. The boss may want you to do a particular task and you may not think that it is productive to do it. Remember the Nike phrase, "Just do it."

You may have a moment at some other time to have a productive conversation with your boss to ask her reasoning for doing the task in the first place, and you may even be able to give your thoughts on why you thought it wasn't productive. If your boss asks you at that point why you didn't speak up before, you could say that it is your job to do the tasks that are asked of you but that in the future, if it is acceptable to the boss, you will certainly raise the issue for purposes of fleshing out all the thoughts behind the proposed task.

Tip #8. Quid Pro Quo Relationship – Interpersonal Reciprocity

> "I'm a mirror. If you're cool with me, I'm cool with you, and the exchange starts. What you see is what you reflect. If you don't like what you see, then you've done something. If I'm standoffish, that's because you are."

> *Jay-Z*

Quid pro quo is the Latin phrase that means "something for something." In other words, it means an exchange of something beneficial, where one transfer is contingent upon the other.

Organizational researchers and psychologists have studied work behavior in the context of the social exchange theory. "According to the theory, individuals engage in a series of interdependent interactions that generate obligations among the exchange parties. When one party provides another with a valued and beneficial resource, an obligation is generated to return a beneficial resource. A series of mutual exchanges strengthens the quality of the relationship between the exchange parties, which thereby produces beneficial and productive behaviors. Empirical evidence supports this pattern. High-quality social exchanges reduce workplace conflict and destructive work behavior."[lvi]

Mara's real world story that best exemplifies this theory involves her relationship with her law partner, Rick Horsch. It was 1992 and the partner for whom Mara worked in the environmental transactional law area abruptly announced that she was leaving their firm to join a competitor firm. Shocked by this news, Mara frantically called all her corporate colleagues and assured them that she, as the lone associate in the environmental group, was ready, willing, and able to handle the environmental issues on all transactions coming into the firm. The firm decided to appoint Rick as the partner in charge of the environmental group and Mara was assigned to teach Rick everything that she knew about the subject matter.

Over the next several years, Rick and Mara worked together to build back the environmental group. The group grew; they expertly serviced their corporate colleagues on environmental issues and worked hard to become experts in the field. Rick always knew that when he called Mara, she would be ready to jump on the new deal. Several years later, she presented her business case to Rick advocating her promotion to Counsel. Believing in her and her commitment to the firm and their practice, Rick sought the necessary approvals for her promotion. In fact, he sought buy-in from Don McNaughton, another beloved partner (socio-political matrix). Together they convinced the managing partner that Mara was deserving of a promotion. Something for something. The key to obtaining the full practicality and benefit of this theory is finding the right people within your place of employment with whom you can have a meaningful exchange. Rick and Mara remain close friends to this day.

Tip #9. The Art of Advocating: Owning Your Career and Creating Your Path

"What is the recipe for successful achievement? To my mind there are just four essential ingredients: Choose a career you love, give it the best there is in you, seize your opportunities, and be a member of the team."

Benjamin Franklin Fairless

Nobody, let us repeat, nobody owns your career. Let's not confuse that with having a boss that tells you what to do or not do. You are the captain of your career ship. You decide what course your career takes, whether to go back to school, gain different experience than you have, change jobs, and so on. We often hear young adults express their expectations that their company will pave the way for a successful career path for them. The flip side of that is that young adults are often disappointed when their company does not do this or that for the advancement of their career. This is a big mistake in thinking.

When Mara got to her law firm in 1987, she knew she wanted to work in the employment area. She went to the office of the partner who did most of that kind of work, Laura Houget, and asked her if she could take off her hands any cases that presented a time-consuming pain for the partner. Laura smiled and handed Mara several EEO claims filed by employees or former employees at various New York branches of foreign banks. Over a short period of time, Mara became the go-to lawyer to handle employment matters at the firm. Two years after she started working at the firm, an announcement was made that the firm needed an associate to work in the environmental transactional area. Not knowing anything about environmental law, Mara raised her hand in hopes that she could create greater job security if she had "two majors" so to speak—employment and environmental law. It worked. She was the lawyer on every deal that came into the office performing environmental and employment due diligence and she had her advisory practice with employment clients. The key was that Mara was motivated to take on as much substantive work as she possibly could in order to gain the requisite experience and become an expert in two areas.

Realistically, motivation is the one true key to success. Successful people are those who can pick themselves up, take a chance, and forge ahead when something needs to be accomplished instead of sitting back, waiting around, or hoping someone will come to you. Perhaps we don't all have the foresight or expertise to see the opportunity or make the right choice from the start of our first jobs. However, if you are a conscientious and logical thinker about what it takes to gain the necessary experience in the field of your choice and you are motivated to go after that experience and have the guts to take calculated risks, you will spot opportunties that others might miss. Take those opportunties. Follow up on every lead you are given or that you identify. Don't sit back and wait for them to come to you.

Tip #10. Ask Smart Questions

"To raise new questions, new possibilities, to regard old problems from a new angle, requires creative imagination and marks real advance in science."

Albert Einstein

A natural instinct in all of us is to speak in order to let others know how smart we are. But if we take the time to listen to others and ask thoughtful questions, we may be perceived as being smarter than if we provided answers. You have to carefully balance this concept of asking smart questions with ensuring that you are not badgering your coworkers or boss with innumerable questions that you could, with some effort, find the answers to on your own. Remember the story of Amy who was asking so many questions that caused her boss to think she was being a pain. *The Harvard Business Review* identified the most effective and empowering questions that create value in one or more of the following ways:

- "They create clarity: "Can you explain more about this situation?"
- They construct better working relations: Instead of "Did you make your sales goal?" ask, "How have sales been going?"
- They help people think analytically and critically: "What are the consequences of going this route?"
- They inspire people to reflect and see things in fresh, unpredictable ways: "Why did this work?"
- They encourage breakthrough thinking: "Can that be done in any other way?"

- They challenge assumptions: "What do you think you will lose if you start sharing responsibility for the implementation process?
- They create ownership of solutions: "Based on your experience, what do you suggest we do here?"[lvii]

Joe, a super-star person and student, graduated from an Ivy League university and applied for a position upon graduation with *Venture for America*, a nonprofit program that places top students at startups in emerging cities. The application process is rigorous, including a team project simulation in which applicants are observed on many criteria. Joe thought he performed masterfully in this simulation, having come up with the idea for the project and getting the team on board for the development of its business strategy and plan for implementation. He did not get the position. The feedback he received was that during the group simulation, he did not encourage others to ask questions or debate the idea, the strategy, or the plan. He essentially skipped over the very important process of allowing others to dissent, ask questions, and voice concerns. Joe really wanted this opportunity and he was not discouraged even after having been denied the position the first time around. Despite the setback, he was motivated to reapply after a year of experience in finance. Joe landed the position on the second go-round, having had a tremendous learning experience about the importance of asking questions, fostering others' participation in the team process, and not always having all the answers.

Tip #11. Build the Business Case for What You Want

> "Some people want it to happen, some wish it would happen, others make it happen."

> *Michael Jordan*

It is not acceptable in business to walk into your boss's office and tell him or her that you want a promotion. You need to build a business case for what you want and this takes hard facts and figures, proven historical record of success, much thought about how you wish to present your case, careful preparation, and the ability to artfully articulate all of what we just said. It is like "leading the horse to water" and doing everything in your power to make the "horse drink that water." You want to present all the facts in a coherent fashion that compels the decision maker or the person who can help influence the decision maker to make the decision that is favorable to you. But wait. We are assuming that you have the gumption to ask. You must ask. That is correct. You must ask for what you want with the appropriate business case to justify it. Of course, your timing in asking for what you want has to be appropriate. Getting counsel from an expert on how to ask for what you want, the timing, and the justification for asking, may be warranted.

Case in point. Mara was eight months pregnant with her son, Noah. It was 1996 and her firm did not have a parental leave policy. Do you recall our discussion of the socio-political matrix? The story we told to depict that theory also depicts the importance of building the business case so we'll get into the weeds on the details. Clearly, Mara had a self-interest in seeing such a policy get implemented fast, but she couldn't let on to that in anything she said and did (despite it being so physically obvious). She had learned that a group of HR folks at the firm was mulling how to craft such a policy and invited Mara to a meeting. She was shocked to learn that the HR folks thought that such a benefit would cost the firm over a quarter million dollars annually, if implemented. There was no way that the firm would adopt such a benefit at that cost. Moreover, she could not comprehend how they had arrived at such a number since they had no data from past experience. She asked them if she could take a crack at drafting and building the business case for adoption of such a policy. They gladly turned it over to her.

For two weeks, Mara worked tirelessly at night after she had put in her twelve billable hours a day and had put her two-year-old to sleep. She requested that HR provide her statistical data for the last three years on associate pregnancies, the number of childbearing female associates, marital status of all associates, and so on. Mara did a competitive analysis of top firms in New York that had such policies, having obtained such information from friends who worked for those competitor firms. She drafted the policy and then, based on the prior three years' statistics, she projected the annual cost of providing such a benefit. The annual projected cost was $72,000. Mara provided a written presentation that included all the data to support the policy, the text of the actual policy, and a com-munications plan to roll out the policy should the firm's management committee approve it. All the work was done. Any smart person reading the presentation would conclude the obvious fact that the firm had been "behind the eight ball" in providing such benefits. That was the more compelling argument for the committee since they were always concerned about recruiting, public perception, and the competition. The parental leave policy was ultimately approved. The key was that Mara did the work, the analysis; she had the data to support her arguments. She went for the ask, and she made it happen by building a solid business case.

Tip #12. Basic Expectations –
What expectation could be problematic?

> "Our environment, the world in which we live and work, is a mirror of our attitudes and expectations."
>
> *Earl Nightingale*

So many people get into trouble or get depressed and become unhappy because their expectations are not being met. That is what our training and message is all about. Know your expectations and evaluate each one of them. They will be different (they should be different) at each step of your career. Identify and evaluate which ones are truly realistic and which ones may not comport with the environment in which you have chosen to "hang your hat." You may need counsel from people more experienced than you in this process. Here's why we say this: it's pretty simple. A recent article picked up by the *Huffington Post* entitled "Why Generation Y Yuppies are Unhappy" featured a simple equation: Happiness = Reality Less Expectations.[lviii] When the reality of someone's life is better than they had expected, they're happy. When reality turns out to be worse than their expectations, they're unhappy. This brings us to our next tip.

Tip #13. The Workplace Is Not Like Home or College

"The greatest discovery of my generation is that a human being can alter his life by altering his attitudes."

William James

One realization that you can make early on is that work is not like home or college life. At home, you may be used to being validated for how smart you are and how good of a person you are. If something doesn't go your way, your parents are often there either to tell you all the reasons why it's ok, emanating sympathy or empathy toward you (despite you thinking that they don't understand), or to highlight that an external factor or person prevented the situation from going your way. At home, your parents may be your best friends. At home, you may feel safe from the pressures of the world. At college, your time is really your own, except for the designated times you're supposed to be in class. Even then, no one cares whether you show up as long as you pass your exams and turn in your papers. Your professors have a sole mission "to engage students of uncommon promise in an intense full-time education of their minds, exploration of their creative faculties and development of their social and leadership abilities, in a four-year course of study and residence" (Bowdoin College Mission Statement). The mission, not unlike many colleges' and universities' missions, is very student-focused. Nobody is concerned about what you wear, you can sleep-in, and you have winter, spring, and summer breaks amounting to approximately twenty-four weeks of vacation. Do you see where we are going with this?

At work, you have to assume that no one will validate how smart you are or how hard you are trying. No one will provide excuses if something for which you are responsible doesn't get done or if something goes wrong. Your boss may not want to be your friend and may not even be a nice person. You have to be on time to work and that time is not of your choosing. There likely is a dress code, albeit business casual. Your time is no longer yours as your vacation will be limited to a certain number of weeks and no more; of course, it may be less if work dictates. The focus is no longer on you. It's on the corporate mission, its customers or clients, the higher-ups, and making money.

Tip #14. Overcome the Needy Presumption

"I don't think it's necessarily healthy to go into relationships as a needy person. Better to go in with a full deck."

Anjelica Huston

We recently presented to a group of organizational development experts and the audience was composed of both Boomer generation experts and Millennial entry-level folks. The discussion revolved around managers' frustration with the level of feedback and approval young adults need. One young person commented in front of the whole group during the question and answer period that the reason for this is, "We will do anything to avoid making a mistake, forget about failure. We loathe the idea of making a mistake or failing. It's simply not happening with our generation." This feeling, which we suspect is fairly universal among young people, is a dangerous one. There was so much implicit and explicit pressure to succeed when you were growing up and a lot of parental protection going on to shield you from failure or setbacks, creating a situation where you need to be validated in order to feel good. Unfortunately, this leads managers and bosses to assume and expect that you will need a lot of hand-holding.

Your conscious focus must be to overcome that presumption of neediness and find validation in simply doing your job and doing it well. You need to alter your expectations that managers, bosses, and senior colleagues are there to guide you through the assignment or tell you how great you are. More often than not, they will not do it. When you get praise or really helpful input from your boss or a senior colleague, you likely will be grateful and appreciative, not to mention surprised. Keep a praise file and put every accolade you get in that file. That way, when you have to do a self-evaluation, you can quote others in their praise of you. There is no question that everyone responds better when given positive feedback and validation. Unfortunately, not every manager or boss understands this. Some corporate cultures are fueled by fear and indifference. There will be time to extract feedback from your senior colleagues during performance review time or after a project is complete. Temper you requests for feedback. The time when you least expect it, you may get it.

Tip #15. Value of the Social Network

"One of the challenges in networking is everybody thinks it's making cold calls to strangers. Actually, it's the people who already have strong trust relationships with you, who know you're dedicated, smart, a team player, who can help you."

Reid Hoffman

Boomer generation business folks marvel at the expansiveness of the social networks of young adults. Having 1,000–2,000 friends or followers on social networks like Facebook or Instagram is the norm rather than the exception for young adults. Young adults must take full advantage of their massive, omnipresent network. Every young adult should start a LinkedIn account. Think about all your friends who have parents working in the industry of your choice. Reach out to those friends and ask them if it would be ok to reach out to their parent for purposes of networking. In our experience, it is rare that people do not want to assist in some way. That doesn't necessarily mean that they will give you a job. But you never know to whom they can refer you. You also will absolutely make headway by contacting people who are alumni of your college or university and reaching out to them. If you are an athlete at your college or university, reach out to alumni athletes. These networks are invaluable and can provide a huge source of contacts and connections.

Noah, Mara's younger son, needed a summer job after his first year of college. His major and minor are economics and computer science, respectively, and he expressed deep interest in the start-up world. One of Mara's closest friends, Mark Weeks, is a venture capital lawyer in San Francisco. Mara asked Mark if he had any start-up clients in New York who needed an intern for the summer. He encouraged Noah to send him a cover letter and resume, which Noah did. Mark passed Noah's resume onto his partner in New York who passed his resume onto his client in New York City. The client, Sailo, reached out to Noah for an interview. It was as if the stars aligned because the company's business is a peer-to-peer marketplace that connects boat owners, captains and renters on one platform.[lix] Noah is a certified sailor and licensed boater! After a Skype interview, Noah landed the internship at Sailo. He was able to combine his academic and career interests in a business that is his passion. This is how networking is supposed to work. It is not necessarily the person you reach out to who will assist you in landing a job. But you never know who they know who could assist you in landing a job.

So what should your introductory email look like? Before he landed his internship, Noah wrote (on his own initiative, we may add) to a father of one of his lacrosse teammates.

Dear Mr. B_____,

By way of introduction, my name is Noah Weissmann and I am a freshman – one of Brian's teammates! Though I have not declared yet, I intend to major in economics and minor in computer science. Throughout my four years of high school at Horace Greeley (one of Scarsdale's rivals!), I maintained a 4.0 GPA with a rigorous course load. Furthermore, during my first semester at Hamilton College, I maintained a 3.85

GPA. Outside of the classroom, as you know, I was recruited as a Division III student-athlete lacrosse goalie. During high school, I was named both a NYS All-American and a NYS Scholar Athlete, both awards being tangible symbols of my strong work ethic and high level of commitment to everything I do inside and outside the classroom.

I understand that I am reaching out to you perhaps a few years in advance. However, as I begin to think about possible options for my summer and, ultimately, my career, I believe any ground-level experience in the business and technology industries would be valuable in helping me to further evaluate where my interests lie. When I talked to Brian about his Intro to Comp Sci class this semester, he mentioned that you have extensive experience and have been working in the tech/computer science field for a while. I would welcome the opportunity to speak with you and learn more about you and your company and how I can best situate myself in years to come to smoothly transition into the business/technology work world.

For your convenience, I have provided you with a copy of my resume. I look forward to speaking with you. I hope to hear from you soon to set up a convenient time for us to talk. See you on the field in a few weeks! Go Continentals!

Sincerely,

Noah Weissmann

Feel free to use the outline (not the details!) of this letter to start reaching out to people in your network. You never know whom they know who can assist you. It will prove to be very valuable to you for not only getting jobs but also for client development.

Tip #16. Dress for Success

"If you look over the years, the styles have changed—the clothes, the hair, the production, the approach to the songs. The icing on the cake has changed flavors. But if you really look at the cake itself, it's really the same."

John Oates

Mara was out to dinner with friends, one of whom is also an attorney and is a tad younger than Mara. The women started talking about what they wore on their first day of their first law firm job. They hysterically laughed at the memory of their bow ties. Yes, bow ties. In the late 80s, female lawyers conformed to the expectation that they would fit in. So, they wore blue skirt suits, white shirts and a bow tie. Mara has a card-key picture to prove it. Three years later, a senior female partner (one of very few), Maureen Donovan, who was the most fashionable person Mara has ever laid eyes on in business and is a lawyer whom Mara respects deeply, wore a pants suit. Male and female lawyers were aghast as she walked by in the cafeteria. Always loving to test the limits in fashion, Mara followed her lead the next day and, voilà, pants suits became in vogue!

So what's the message? Dressing for success is critical. It can make or break you. Clothes say a lot about who we are and our self-confidence. We suggest that you go to a store like Brooks Brothers and invest in your first set of essential business clothes. You can always supplement your business wardrobe with less expensive clothes as you earn more disposable income.

Business casual can be misleading. We always advise our young adult clients to take it a notch above what they think everyone else will wear and what your company policy dictates. That said, you need to conform to the "letter of the law" on the dress code—never take it down a notch.

When you have an interview or client meeting, for women, dresses and solid color skirts with silk blouses are chic. Pants with a tailored jacket and blouse are always neat and clean-cut. Take a cue from your organization about whether open-toed shoes are acceptable (no flip-flops or sandals). Mara was the policy drafter for what constituted acceptable open-toed shoes at a major accounting firm after the Director of HR was sitting in an airport and wrote an email to his staff that he was "seeing open-toed shoes everywhere … What does this mean? Is this the latest shoe fashion? What are we to do with our dress code shoe policy?"

Men should wear pressed pants (khakis are acceptable), belt, *polished* shoes, and pressed shirts. Always wear a suit for a client meeting. It's not just about the clothes you wear. Your grooming is essential, as well. As a lawyer, Mara often gets the question about what to do with an employee who is not well groomed. Hair, deodorant, fragrances (nothing potent!), nails, and facial hair are all things that need to be tended to and groomed for the business world.

Tip #17. Email Etiquette

"There are four ways, and only four ways, in which we have contact in the world. We are evaluated and classified by these four contacts: what we do, how we look, what we say, and how we say it."

Dale Carnegie

Salutations and Subject Matter

Just like what we wear, we are constantly evaluated in business by what we say, both orally and in writing. We worked with a college professor who spoke about how outraged she was over being addressed by a student in an email with "Hey Prof, ..." It's simply unacceptable in business to start any email with "Hey." "Yo" is out of the question, as well. Salutations in business should always assume that business communications are formal, unless you are told otherwise. Start with "Dear ..." As for using Mr. or Ms. and a last name, we believe that you should inquire what is acceptable. Business is often on a first name basis, although in Mara's law firm, the senior most partners were always addressed as Mr. and Ms. at first. When corresponding with foreign colleagues and/or clients, you should use a more formal salutation unless told otherwise. Make sure you always put a subject line as many people categorize their e-files by the subject matter. You will find that how fast you get a response will depend on your subject line.

Adding the email addresses of the intended recipients can be tricky. It is so easy to send your email to the wrong person and, with confidentiality of information, this could be really troublesome. Always insert the addressee(s) last and make sure you have the correct intended recipients.

Content—Start with a Warm and Personal Note Depending on the Context

It is so easy to start right into your email with the substance of the business information you need to convey or the questions you need to ask. We always do that: jump right in and get right to the point. Invariably, we circle back to the start of our emails and write, "I hope this email finds you well" or something of a personal touch. It certainly will depend on the context but it is a good check on email etiquette to ask yourself whether the email sounds inviting of a response and whether it will motivate the receiver to get the information that you need to finish your assignment.

CCs, BCCs and Reply to All

Be very sensitive whom you address in your CCs. We have been on email chains where the entire world is copied and this can be problematic on a number of levels depending on the content of the email. Use blind copy most sparingly as it is not cool to talk behind people's backs and BCCs are comparable to that. You are letting some other person know of your communication with your recipient and that recipient is not aware that the conversation is a three-way conversation. Moreover, you run the risk that the other person does not recognize that they are blind copied and shoots back an email by replying to all. This could be embarrassing, depending on the content. The message is clear. Do not be quick to use these tools without full comprehension of what can go wrong.

Who Owns the Technology?

The technology that you are provided to do your job is not yours. To understand the world of business technology, you must totally understand that the company you work for owns the technology it provides you to do your job. That means that anything you write, send, circulate, and search on the Internet is the company's domain, and the company has the unfettered right to snoop and review. The essential rule of thumb is do not send personal emails from your company email, do not view sites that are inappropriate from your company computer, do not send your company's confidential information to your private computer, do not send jokes around, and do not write emails that you would not want to appear on the front page of *The Wall Street Journal*.

Tip #18. Giving and Accepting Criticism

"Criticism may not be agreeable, but it is necessary. It fulfills the same function as pain in the human body. It calls attention to an unhealthy state of things."

Winston Churchill

No one likes to hear that they did something wrong. If we only knew that we would all be safe in our jobs despite being criticized for not doing something right, perhaps we would be able to take the criticism better. Unfortunately, that is not the case. Young adults loathe the idea of failing or making a mistake. Remember the story of Amy. She was distraught that her boss was abrupt with her and told her that the question she asked was a dumb one. Amy was so busy trying to make a good impression on her boss that she was like a gnat buzzing around his head as she asked question after question. He was annoyed that she couldn't figure things out on her own. After being coached, Amy expressed to her boss that she felt belittled when he told her that her question was dumb, and that she hoped he would appreciate how hard she was working. She agreed that she needed to find out answers to questions independent of him (demonstrating self-awareness, accountability, and acknowledgment of criticism) but told him she hoped he would be open to mentoring her. This strategy earned her very positive feedback in the way she handled upward feedback (giving criticism) and her ability to accept responsibility for her role in the situation.

Interestingly, when asked whether they needed to build their strengths or fix their weaknesses in order to succeed professionally, 73% of Millennial respondents chose to focus on their weaknesses—a much higher proportion than older generations.[ix] The difficulty is that not every person giving criticism gives it constructively or with respect, causing the receiver of the criticism to be angry and defensive and to believe the critic is rude and off base.

The key is to:

- Dispel all judgments, negative or otherwise, about the person giving you the criticism;
- Handle all responses to criticism with grace and show appreciation to the person for taking time to give the criticism;
- Thank the person for the criticism and acknowledge that it is helpful in your training/learning;
- Express a desire to do a good job and a willingness to learn where things went wrong and where they could be better;
- Acknowledge what you could have done better;
- Offer to take another crack at the project; do whatever it takes to make it better.

Tip #19. Possess a Client Service Mentality (Internal and External)

"Service to others is the rent you pay for your room here on earth."

Muhammad Ali

Mara's son, Gabriel, was six years old and in first grade when Mara started working from home on Fridays. She did this mostly because Gabe's first grade teacher demanded parental assistance in class one hour a week. Gabe often came into Mara's home office when he returned from school and saw her with her ear to the phone and her index finger raised as if to say "just one minute." The one minute invariably turned into ten minutes, but he knew that his mother was on the phone with a client (she mouthed it to him) and so he had to patiently wait for her to finish tending to her client's needs. This was a very common scene on Fridays. When Gabe was about eight, Mara and her husband asked him what he wanted to be when he grew up. Without skipping a beat, he proclaimed that he wanted to be a client.

Gabe saw how his mom's attention was unequivocally on her client. Harvey and Mara have both had the fortune of having external, client-facing careers as well as operational careers (non-external clients). Fortunately for them, they had decades of client service experience before they took on operational roles. When they took on the operational roles, they instinctively viewed their colleagues—those in business roles in the company—as their clients. Yes, they were internal clients and no, they didn't pay a fee for their advice. But in terms of how Mara and Harvey viewed their roles, they fundamentally believed that those business people who ran the business units or departments had needs and they were in their roles to serve them.

As a professional with a client/customer service mentality, you will have to demonstrate many of the attributes we have discussed in this book. Certainly, you need to have empathy and step into the shoes of your client in order to understand what they need and how they feel. You have to be enthusiastic (whether you like your client or not) that they are calling upon you to do a task for them. You have to be resilient because there may come a time when the "client" is distressed and takes it out on you or is upset that you did not do something fast enough for them. Clients can be very demanding. You have to be responsive and responsible in order to earn their trust and compel them to call upon you every time they need something. You have to be adaptable because often the client changes course or doesn't know what he/she needs or doesn't know what he doesn't know, and it will be up to you to think out of the box in order to educate the client.

This is a mentality that is crucial to acquire for ultimate success. Whether you are in a service business with clients or customers or in an operational, administrative, or strategic role, view your internal and/or external constituents as your clients for whom you are giving of yourself and providing a valuable service.

Tip #20. Possess a Sense of Urgency

"I have been impressed with the urgency of doing. Knowing is not enough; we must apply. Being willing is not enough; we must do."

Leonardo da Vinci

A client once asked Mara, "How much time has to pass before I send a thank you note to my interviewer?" Mara wrote back, "Send immediately." Urgency is a state of mind not a process. This sense of urgency is not a frenetic, panicky, anxious state of being; rather, it is a progressive, spirited, engaged mindset that propels you to respond in a timely manner, move ideas along, and be in an "on-switch" mode in your work world. Your teammates and bosses should never have to wonder where projects stand with you. When you receive an email with a question, don't wait a few hours or a day to answer it. Be proactive and answer it as expeditiously as you can. If you are focused on the task at hand, you will avoid distractions and will better understand what is needed to attain the desired results. This may sound elementary, but people are often successful not because they are the smartest ones in the room but because they possess a sense of urgency for getting things done and being responsive to others. Deadlines help a person set goals and meet them in a timely fashion but without a sense of urgency, it is easy to miss steps along the way or miss opportunities to communicate with the powers that be. Herein lies the distinction between having urgency because of something external creating a need for you to move forward (a deadline, for example) versus having a sense of urgency that comes from your internal composition. Develop your own internal sense of urgency in order to take the necessary action steps to attain your desired outcomes.

This internal drive to move things forward must be balanced carefully with an understanding of what tasks are most important to accomplish with a driving desire. As John Kotter suggests in his book, *A Sense of Urgency*, leaders need to instill a sense of urgency in their workers because without it, mediocrity and complacency prevail and mediocrity and complacency are not the stuff that successful change is made of. Instead, they are the key ingredients for failure.

Exercise #3 Create your own SharpenUrEdge™ tip

Create your own SharpenUrEdge™ tip. You can do this by asking yourself what you expect from your job. What are the differences between your job expectations and the expectations that people in other generations (Traditionalists, Boomers, Gen X) have of you?

PART 3 –
Knowing Yourself and Influencing Others

Chapter 5

Getting Out of the
Comfort Zone: Know Yourself

It is important to know yourself and the value you bring to the table. Until you get to know the ropes of the work world, you're likely to feel a bit scared, out of place, insecure, and uncomfortable. The temptation is to retreat into your known world and pretend that everything is OK. This is not a good strategy. Finding out about the world of work is a job in itself. It requires not only motivation, but preparation, practice, and curiosity. It also helps if you know what kind of job you're looking for, but that is not what this book is about. We're going to assume that you have some idea of the kind of role you are after and in what industry you want to start your career. It's what you do about it that is the topic here.

Gearing Up for the World of Work

As you gear up for the work world, it is important to learn about yourself through self-awareness, something that many people go through life never doing. Understanding how one is perceived by the rest of the world is often what separates those who are truly successful from those who are not.

You are probably thinking that you know a lot of successful people who haven't a clue about themselves or those around them and couldn't care less about how the rest of the world perceives them. Ask them how that is working for them. For sure, they do not know just how many people they have "left for dead" on the road to their success.

A sense of self-awareness causes one to stop and think, "What can I do better? What is my contribution to this situation?" We can spend a lot of good energy talking about how others treat us or how they fall short. The bottom line is that we have no control over how others behave. We do, however, have control over how we act, respond, and react.

We Can Only Change Our Own Behaviors
But to Do That We Must Be Self-Aware

Self-awareness is "the capacity for introspection and the ability to recognize oneself as an individual separate from the environment and other individuals."[lxi] Self-awareness sets us up to modify our behavior when things in our environment are not going according to plan. When you encounter problems or become dissatisfied with a situation with which you are presented at work, being self-aware will cause you to see *your role* in a given situation and see the facts of the situation for what they are, to cognitively think through what *you* can do about it, and mentally, to believe that *you* are capable of making a change. You may very well be able to visualize a better situation. You may then be motivated to put *your plan* into action. Our focus is on helping you understand your expectations for the work world and where those expectations may diverge from the expectations that the workplace and those for whom you will be working have for you. Again, to do this effectively, you need a sense of self-awareness. The reason why we are going through this exercise is to help you do your part to bridge the gap between the perceptions others have of you and the expectations you have for your career, your colleagues, bosses, and work, in general. Simply put, your success and happiness will be determined by how well you bridge the gap between what you expect from your employer and what your employer expects from you.

The Johari Window

Here's one place to start exploring yourself and your value. It's called Exploring Room 3, and here's the reason why. Back in 1955 when the thought of electronic devices that permanently connected people to each other was the fantasy of crazy scientists and sci-fi shows, two psychologists, Joseph Luft and Harrington Ingram, developed a matrix to help people explore themselves, both through their own eyes and through the eyes of others. It's called the Johari Window, sometimes referred to as the house with four rooms.

	Known to self	*Not known to self*
Known to others	Room 1 The Arena	Room 2 Blind Spot
Not known to others	Room 4 Façade	Room 3 The Unknown

Figure 1 The Johari Window

Room 1 is the part of ourselves that we see and that others see. It is the known world.

Room 2 is the aspects of ourselves that others see but we are not aware of. It is our blind spot. Close friends may tell you things about yourself that you either don't see in yourself or deny exist.

Room 3 is the most mysterious room in that it contains the vast unknown ... unknown to ourselves and to others ... the place of great danger and great opportunity.

Room 4 is our private space that we keep hidden from others.

Exercise #4

Create a table like this and fill in as much information as you can in each room. To do this, you may need to talk to people you know who would be willing to provide honest feedback about how you come across to them, things about you that are known to them but not to you. The purpose of examining the Johari Window is to ultimately reduce the size of Room 3 and increase the size of Room 1.

What Kind of Behavioral Style Do You Have? The Four Social Types

Another place for self-exploration/self-understanding is with a look at your social (or behavioral) style(s). Before going into details about the four varying social styles, we'd like you to take a small test. Because you are answering these questions about yourself, you may want to consider the results with more than a couple grains of salt. It has been reported that about 50% of people misrepresent themselves in this type of self-take test.

Exercise #5

Place a check mark on the dash mark next to each word that you feel describes you. If it doesn't apply to you, do not put a check mark. Add up the number of marks under each column. The results are described below. Some of the results may not be a surprise to you … on the other hand … Here Be Monsters.

	A	B	C	D
Critical	_			
Comforting		_		
Manipulating			_	
Pushy				_
Indecisive	_			
Unsure		_		
Excitable			_	
Severe				_
Stuffy	_			
Ingratiating		_		
Undisciplined			_	
Tough				_
Picky	_			
Dependent		_		
Reacting			_	
Dominating				_
Moralistic	_			
Awkward		_		
Egotistical			_	
Harsh				_

Industrious	_		
Supportive		_	
Ambitious			_
Strong Willed				_
Persistent	_		
Respectful		_	
Stimulating			_
Independent				_
Serious	_		
Willing	_		
Enthusiastic			_
Practical				_
Expecting	_		
Dependable		_	
Dramatic			_
Decisive				_
Orderly	_		
Agreeable		_	
Social			_
Efficient				_
Totals: A ____	B ____	C ____	D ____

Add up your score for each column. Chances are that you will have a higher score for one of these columns than for the other three.

A – The Analytic: You perceive yourself to be an Analytical person. Analyticals are essentially perfectionists, people who serve no wine, take no precipitous action, before its time. The very best thing about Analyticals is that, nine times out of ten, they are right about things because they gave the matter their time, reflection, and rational consideration and have done vast amounts of research and data gathering. Their strong suit is the facts. Their key virtue is patience, and it may also be their downfall. They show a kind of caution that paralyzes, not from fear but from a determination to fully understand a problem before moving toward a solution. Pushed to the brink, the Analytical will usually run for cover until the shooting stops. However, Analyticals are able to carry huge loads in a steady and straightforward manner. While most people consider Analyticals to be introverts, it is possible to be an extroverted Analytical, someone who chases others down the hall quoting facts, figures, reasons, and contraindications. They are 100 percent social with matters that most people don't consider social fodder.

B – The Amiable: You perceive yourself to be an Amiable person. You go where the wind takes you. Amiables are essentially people people, considerate and very empathic. They are the warm fuzzies of the world. Their orientation is the past, present, and the future— wherever people have needs and may be hurt. They are the world's best coordinators, precisely because they take time to touch base with all parties. Sure, they have opinions, but they may be more interested to know yours. Their great strength is their understanding of relationships. Pushed to the brink, their response is usually to cave in. While most people consider Amiables to be introverts, there are extroverted Amiables. Be wary of the extroverted Amiable as they will want to be with you so much they make you want to move to another state.

C – The Expressive: You perceive yourself to be an Expressive person. Like a cruise ship, parties and fancy tablecloths are the norm. Expressives are big-picture people, always looking for a fresh perspective on the world around them. They are future-oriented, perhaps because that is where no one can ever pin them down as they dream their grand dreams. If you want a straight answer, Expressives may not be the best place to turn. If you want intuition and creativity, they're wonderful. If you want a terrific party, invite lots of Expressives. Pushed to the brink, Expressives can react savagely, by attacking. Though cheerful, they take the world they create in their heads seriously. While most people consider Expressives to be extroverts, you may be an introverted Expressive. You can recognize them coming down the hall, smiling, whistling a tune, high as a kite. Inside they're having a party, but no one else is invited to it.

D – The Driver: Forceful and direct, you perceive yourself to be a Driver. Drivers are essentially let-me-do-it people. They are firmly rooted in the present moment, and they are lovers of action. Their great strength is results. If you want to discuss a job, talk to one of the other three types; if you just want it done, take it to a Driver. They aren't much for inner exploration, but they sure bring home the bacon. They can be bitterly self-critical and resentful of idle chitchat. Their favorite song is "Steamroller Blues." Pushed to the brink, Drivers become tyrants. While most people see Drivers as extroverts, it is possible to be an introverted Driver. They are leaders by nature, but not sharers. Instead of driving others, they drive themselves and are prone to workplace illnesses, migraines, workaholism, and high gastrointestinal awareness. [lxii]

The Key to Becoming More Versatile: Understanding Others with the Four Keys: What, Why, Who, and How

Now that you are equipped with an understanding of what social type you are, you can use these same descriptors to ascertain the social types of those with whom you work (your boss, colleagues, clients, and customers). In this chapter, we provide you with an overview of what each social type wants to hear and a guide to what you need to say/not say/do/not do when dealing with each social type. This understanding will help you influence others by tailoring your interactions with them based on their way of receiving information and processing data. You will achieve more success if you focus on the person to whom you are presenting or with them and theirs. Ted Goff, once again, depicts this concept beautifully in his cartoon:

"What do you mean 'no'? I don't understand that word. Are you trying to say 'yes' in some delightfully new way?"

What Drivers want to hear: Since Drivers are outcome-oriented, they want to hear that you are the same. They want to hear "What" you are trying to accomplish, what is the outcome you're shooting for. They want to know that you have your eyes focused on specific results.

What Expressives want to hear: Since Expressives are future-oriented, they want to hear that you have a rationale for your actions that have an impact on future results. "Why" are you taking the actions you are taking, for what future purpose?

What Amiables want to hear: Since Amiables are people people, they want to know "Who" you have talked to, who is involved in the data gathering, who you are talking to, who will use the results of your data gathering, and who will be impacted by the outcomes of your actions. They will want to know the opinions and comments of those with whom you have spoken.

What Analyticals want to hear: Since Analyticals are data driven, they want to know the process that you will use to come to a solution. "How" will you get to the results, what specific steps will you be taking to get the results you want?

Dealing with Drivers:

- Be brief and to the point. Think efficiency.
- Stick to business. Skip the chitchat. Close loopholes. Dispel ambiguities. Digress at your peril. Speculate and you're history.

- Be prepared. Know the requirements and objectives of the task at hand.
- Organize your arguments into a neat package. Present your facts cleanly and logically.
- Be courteous, not chummy. Don't be bossy; Drivers do not let themselves be driven.
- Ask specific questions. Don't go fishing for answers.
- If you disagree, disagree with the facts, not the person.
- If you agree, support the results and the person.
- Persuade by citing objectives and results. Outcomes rule!
- When finished, leave. No loitering.

Dealing with Expressives:

- Meet their social needs while talking shop. Entertain, stimulate, be lively.
- Talk about their goals as well as yours.
- Be open; strong and silent does not cut it with Expressives.
- Take time. They are most efficient when not in a hurry.
- Ask for their opinions and ideas.
- Keep your eye on the big picture, not the technical details.
- Support your points with examples involving people they know and respect.
- Offer special deals, extras, incentives.
- Show honest respect; you must not talk down to an Expressive.

Dealing with Amiables:

- Break the ice; it shows your commitment to the task and to them.
- Show respect. Amiables will be hurt by any attempt to patronize.
- Listen and be responsive. Take your time. Learn the whole story.
- Be nonthreatening, casual, and informal. A crisp, commanding style will send Amiables packing.
- Ask *how* questions to draw out their opinion.
- Define what you want them to contribute to the task.
- Assure and guarantee that the decision at hand will in no way risk, harm, or threaten others, but make no assurances you can't back up.

Dealing with Analyticals:

- Prepare your case in advance.
- Take your time but be persistent.
- Support their principles. Show you value their thoughtful approach.
- Cover all bases. Do not leave things to chance or hope something good will happen.
- Draw up a scheduled approach for any action plan. Be specific on roles and responsibilities.
- Be clear. Disorganization or sloppiness in presentation is a definite turn-off.
- Avoid emotional arguments. No wheedling or cajoling. No

pep rallies.
- Follow through. The worst thing you can do with an Analytical is break your word, because they will remember.

You can choose to target a specific person by modifying your communication approach based on your perception of their type. This is called being versatile. Or, you can do what's called broadcast versatility. This is where you include in your conversation with any one person (or group of people) all four basic response needs as described above. For example, in the conversation, you work in "what" is going to happen, "why" you are doing it, "how" you are going about achieving the goal, and "who" is either using the outcome or providing the input. That way, no matter what the other person's behavioral style is at the moment, you will hit their communication needs.

Which Mindset Are You?

The psychologist Carol Dweck has done research on and identified two types of mindsets that determine how well you are able to cope successfully with work—and life. They are the Fixed Mindset and the Growth Mindset. The Fixed Mindset person believes that our destinies are pretty much predetermined by our intelligence and history. We have a certain amount of gray matter that only has so much capacity. If we're dumb, we stay dumb. If we're smart, we remain smart. The problem with the Fixed Mindset is that it sets up the need to defend one's capabilities and continuously affirm one's status. "I need to prove over and over that I'm smart, and I need for you to affirm my opinion by telling me so." A Fixed Mindset person believes that what you were is what you are and you cannot change that. You cannot do what you are incapable of because your assets are fixed.

The Growth Mindset, however, believes in continuous learning and growth and believes that it is important to ask for and receive feedback as a way of seeking continuous improvement. Let us be clear here. We are not talking about sitting cross-legged on some mountaintop humming chants to your inner gods. We are talking about getting things done, achieving outcomes, in a nonjudgmental atmosphere. We are talking about improving continuously, learning from your failures, working with others to achieve team successes—the *we* instead of the *me*.

In all generations, both mindsets exist. What is unique about young adults is that while you are known to have received copious praise and, therefore, are said to have unrealistic expectations of your capabilities (that is not us saying this, but the researchers—please don't shoot the messenger), young adults today have an overwhelming desire to take on challenges, get better, and learn continuously. Young adults are said to have the entitlement gene, but what we believe you feel entitled to are opportunities to grow, learn, receive feedback, and contribute along with colleagues and leaders who share a similar Growth Mindset.

Young adults are turned off by supervisors/leaders with fixed mindsets who set standards that are sometimes too low or who sit in judgment of all things around them, slotting people into categories of competence. Leaders who support some and ignore others and leaders who feel the need to protect their position and stifle opportunities for others to grow and learn are not high on young adults' list of favorites. Growth Mindset leaders seek opportunities as challenges and failure as places of learning while Fixed Mindset leaders protect their rears by avoiding difficult challenges that may result in mistakes or failure and may challenge their position of superiority. Growth Mindset leaders believe that things can change and develop while Fixed Mindset leaders think in terms of labels, fixed talent, qualities, and characteristics.

How Growth Drivers Behave: Drivers with growth mindsets push for results and action and look for opportunities to challenge the status quo. They set lofty goals and high expectations. When failure occurs, they don't blame but look for ways to learn from the mistakes and make themselves and their teams more effective.

How Fixed Drivers Behave: They push for results and take action without taking very many risks. Risks mean higher levels of failures, which cannot be tolerated. Heads roll when mistakes are made. They avoid taking on unknown challenges and choose safer, more certain pathways.

How Growth Expressives Behave: They push the boundaries of creativity and seek new and unique outcomes. Failures are just a part of doing business and they believe that, as Gore Vidal was quoted as saying, "The only place success comes before work is in the dictionary." They work hard, play hard, and don't let failures get them down. After all, it took Thomas Edison over 1000 trials before he discovered the correct filament to use for his new electric light bulb. Tenacity is what Growth Expressives are all about. They seek a greater understanding of why things operate the way they do and how they can do things differently.

How Fixed Expressives Behave: They follow a formula for trying things out. While they are very trial-and-error oriented, they are not as tenacious as the Growth Expressives. They seem surprised that trying the same way over and over again results in the same outcomes. They may use different variables, but the method is the same, resulting in less than optimum outcomes. They believe in the creativity of the method even while the method used is the same over and over again.

How Growth Analyticals Behave: Growth Analyticals look for different methods that produce the same outcomes to verify that the outcomes are correct. They experiment with different ways of achieving the outcomes that they can create and then codify. They sometimes drive people nuts with their continuous changing of policies and procedures.

How Fixed Analyticals Behave: Fixed Analyticals have only one pathway. Once the process is established, you follow the process precisely. They love policies and procedures but don't modify them as often as is sometimes needed.

How Growth Amiables Behave: Growth Amiables look for continuous ways of increasing the scope and depth of communication and teamwork within an organization. They create avenues for individuals to become engaged in the team process and for everyone to know what's going on all the time. They feel bad when someone doesn't want to join in or take advantage of the opportunities to grow that are provided by the organization.

How Fixed Amiables Behave: They have a fixed group of people that they engage with on a regular basis and, while open to this group, are often somewhat standoffish (closed) to strangers from outside their group.

The Leadership Kaleidoscope

If you've ever looked through a kaleidoscope, you know how wonderful it can be. The images create a rainbow of color and design. Just a twist and the next image is a new view of the same content. We can get a different view of a young adult's mindset if we twist the kaleidoscope a bit from the Growth vs. Fixed Mindset to one we'll call Radiators vs. Drains.

Radiators are individuals who believe in getting the best out of everyone. They breathe engagement and support the dreams and desires of others (bosses, peers, and subordinates). People are drawn to Radiators like moths to fire. They make people feel accomplished and worthwhile. They generate joy at work and have a willingness to help teammates succeed.

Drains are those people who also radiate, but they radiate toxic fumes. They could be wearing one of those radiation-warning signs around their necks. While their toxic levels may vary, one thing they have in common is their determination to interfere with progress. They drain the energy from an organization by promoting the status quo, challenging change, and avoiding risk or punishing those who take risk. Fear of the unknown is a constant. They operate out of fear of failure. They may have experienced failure or punishment in the past and don't want to get knocked down again. When they are in leadership positions, they lead by invoking fear in others.

Young adults today, very generally speaking, tend to be in the Radiator category and don't understand the mindset of those who drain the life out of an organization. The best thing a young adult can do to help those who are drains to the organization is to encourage them (or others who can help them) to get included on teams that are working on new and exciting enterprises and to reward their efforts as well as their outcomes in order to break their self-defeating mental state.

Another way of assessing mindset is to look at something called the numerator/denominator factor. There are only two ways to get a bigger result from a fraction; either increase the top number (numerator) or decrease the bottom number (denominator). Numerator leaders try to get better outcomes by increasing risk-taking, engaging in creativity, endorsing positive changes, promoting continuous learning, and simply by doing more. Denominator leaders try to get better outcomes by restricting risk-taking, reducing new product development, cutting resources like training, cutting payroll, and drawing back programs.

As an example, Harvey did some work for Toro Company years

ago. Just before he started working with them, they had a culture of brutality so the message was clear: don't take any chances. If you took a chance and were wrong, you could expect to get fired or have your responsibilities restricted. It was a stressful workplace. Then Ken Melrose was elevated to the CEO role. He wanted to change the culture from denominator to numerator. He called all-employee meetings regularly to let everyone know how his plans for positive change were coming along. Not much happened until he put action behind his words. Two engineers wanted to take a chance and create a new type of disposable lawn mower using a unique manufacturing process of blown fiber. Remember, the old culture was that if you made a mistake, you could expect to see your belongings in a box on the curb. Well, these engineers took the risk because they believed in the new product's possibilities. As it turned out, there were major problems with the new technique and the project was an abysmal failure, costing about $8 million. Afterwards, these two engineers started hiding, keeping their heads down, and hoping no one would notice them.

Three months later, just as they began to breathe a bit easier, they were called to Ken Melrose's office. "Holy crap," they thought, "we're done now for sure." They hadn't worked together since this project went south. They looked at each other empathetically in Ken's outer office before they were invited inside. When they went inside, they saw balloons, streamers, cake, punch; it looked like a party. When they meekly asked what the decorations were for, Ken said that they were for these two engineers. Not as a celebration of their departure, but as a celebration of their risk-taking. Ken told them that even though he was not happy with the loss of revenue, he was celebrating their willingness to try new things, build new products, expand their offerings. He told them that he wanted them to keep innovating. And even though there would be failures, the successes would outweigh the losses and the company would grow as a result. "Now go back to work and help us grow." The engineers were stunned, speechless, and left Ken's office reenergized. How long do you think that story took to circulate throughout the company and make people believe that the new culture of innovation and growth would work? Toro grew from about $400 million to over $2 billion in revenue. Ken was a numerator leader.

Exercise #6 – What Color Is Your Kaleidoscope?

Imagine you're looking into your kaleidoscope. What you see at first is your usual way of seeing the world, making the distinctions that matter to you. Now you are going to twist the kaleidoscope to change your perception, to see things according to the distinctions we've made above.

> Twist: Growth Mindset vs. Fixed Mindset
>
> Twist: Radiator vs. Drain
>
> Twist: Optimist vs. Pessimist
>
> Twist: Numerator vs. Denominator

For each twist, identify which side of the polarity you most resemble and write an introspective paragraph about why you think you are one type and not the other. Are there some contexts in which you change your preferences?

Chapter 6

There Be Monsters: Tacking Against the Headwinds and Rough Seas

Conflict in the Workplace, Really?

The world would be a much better, calmer, more peaceful place if everyone would just get along, right? First and foremost, workers at all levels must learn to accept conflict as an inevitable part of their work environment. The *CPP Global Human Capital Report* (2008) study found that an overwhelming majority (85%) of employees at all levels experience conflict to some degree. Furthermore, it was determined through this study that U.S. employees spend 2.8 hours per week dealing with conflict, equating to approximately $359 billion in paid hours in 2008.[lxiii]

There are many contributors to conflict in the workplace: interpersonal relationships, differences in social style, power struggles, interdependence conflicts, and differences in gender, background, and culture. People and systems are pretty much designed to conflict with each other on a number of planes. The most common disagreements/conflicts are:

Personality conflicts/Toxic relationships

You've been there. You want to move ahead with a decision. You have all the information that you need to pull the trigger. But, Lisa, your boss/colleague/team member doesn't agree. She needs more information, more time, more, more. She doesn't feel comfortable that all the details have been worked out yet and is too hesitant to make a decision. Drives you nuts! You've just witnessed a very common toxic relationship. You have an Expressive and an Analytical trying to do what they feel/think is the right thing but they go about making their decisions based on their very different personalities. Similarly, Driver and Amiable personalities have a naturally occurring toxic relationship. Thankfully, most young adults today are good collaborators and the resistance that is present in a toxic relationship is reduced to the point of minor annoyance rather than crossed swords.

Conflicts around goals/objectives

There are times in any organization when in order to get your team's goals accomplished, some other team's top priority may have to wait to get done. You may need to borrow some of their resources (especially if your goal is higher on the company's overall priority list). Much of the time, one team's goals don't conflict with other teams; you run parallel toward a common outcome. There are times, however, when goals conflict. In that case, the natural tendency of young adults is to attempt negotiation to resolve conflict. This is an ideal path to follow. If, however, emotions get involved and tempers flare, you may need to bring in a third person (or a supervisor) to mediate.

Conflicts around roles/responsibilities

Who's responsible for what, by when, and how are you going to check with each other to make sure you're on the same page? As people fulfill their job responsibilities and take on more/different tasks, it is important to ask this question regularly to avoid an unintended conflict over roles. "I thought that was my job." "No, that's my job, not yours." Also, there are those who want to enhance their skills and take on "other" responsibilities in the process. Apprenticeships can be used to allow a person to "try out" and "learn" add-on skills (under the eyes of a mentor) to benefit themselves, the team, and the overall organization.

Conflicts with leadership style

Let's face it, there are good leaders and those who seem like they're the devil's spawn. If you are dealing with "normal" people in a leadership role (keeping in mind that about 5 percent of the population are genuinely crazy), they are trying to do their best. Their style of leadership (based somewhat on personalities) can vary and run into toxic leadership styles similar to toxic interpersonal relationships.

Conflicts between personal values and culture

If we stay with the toxic relationship theme, there are four cultures that leaders create in their companies. Again, these are based in part on their personalities. Driver personalities tend to create Pummel (my way or the highway) cultures. Analyticals tend to create Push (scare you with data) cultures. Expressives tend to create Pull (vision of the future) cultures. Amiables tend to create Pamper (hold no one accountable) cultures. So, it's possible for two leaders in the same unit to create conflicting cultures based on their conflicting personalities. Versatility is the key to overcoming conflicting leadership styles. There are also potential conflicts between your personal values and the values of the organization. Harvey knew a woman who was an antiwar protester in the 70s. She was excited to be recruited to work in human resources for Honeywell. You know, "Mother Honeywell," maker of thermostats and sensors—how harmless. Once she learned that Honeywell was also one of the biggest manufactures of bombs, bullets, and torpedoes, she couldn't get out the door fast enough. Her personal values clashed with the values of the company. Young adults, today, care deeply about corporate responsibility and larger companies know this and have made corporate responsibility a large part of their overall long-term strategy.

Conflicts between personal needs and organizational needs

No one works on a team unless they feel that they are getting their personal needs met along the way toward meeting the team's goals. So, it's important to let others/leaders know what needs you have (e.g., learning a new piece of software, flexing your working hours, getting equal pay, etc.) and see if it's possible to have them met. This, of course, should be conveyed after you have some (successful) tenure with your company and you have earned some good will (remember our discussion about giving of yourself to your organization when you start out). You only get what you ask for. If you don't tell your leader what you need, you may not get it. There are times, however, when there is a conflict between what you need from the organization and what the organization needs from you. You may feel that your needs/interests are at odds with the organization's needs/interests, but this is an assumption that you need to test out. It is possible/likely that your two interests are different but not in conflict with each other. A willingness to negotiate to get both needs/interests met goes a long way toward satisfying these differing needs.

Buccaneers and Barnacles: A Taxonomy of Bad Bosses

So here they are ... Bad Bosses.[lxiv] We have several names for them. We do not want to scare you. We want you to be aware that they exist and give you tools to deal with, and be successful under, them.

The Micromanager

> This boss controls the thoughts and actions of her subordinates. Often, it could be a result of an overinflated sense of self (no one is as good and smart as I am) or the boss's insecurities. It will take a while to gain the trust of a micromanager. The key is for you not to take actions that will be interpreted by the micromanager as insubordinate even if you think that you are doing the job for which you are hired to do. Let the boss direct you until you have "earned the right" in her mind to act more independently.

The Bully Boss

> You really have to decipher whether the bully boss, if you

have one, is really psychotic (in which case, you need to do what you can to change roles or get a new job) or simply a person who rules by intimidation. This is not an easy distinction to make. You actually can approach a boss who does not have pathological characteristics but simply has an inflated sense of power and authority and feels more competent when she points out the weaknesses in and mistakes of others (this is where you may need a consultation with Harvey!). Once you determine your boss is the latter type, you can, like our client, Amy, did with her boss, approach the boss with a well-thought-through script to let him know how you feel when he bullies you.

The Nervous Nelly

This boss is constantly worried —about the work, his job, the department, customers, the numbers, the profits, deadlines, and office politics. The effect is that others who work with this boss can easily get nervous and paralyzed as well. You may be able to be helpful by engaging him in a discussion about what he thinks the triggers are for his nervousness. It's tricky because you do not want him to be defensive and you do not want to appear cavalier. You have to work hard to ensure your nervous boss that you are doing everything to get the job done in as expert a way as you know how. Adding a few "don't worry . . ." comments before you give updates may also be helpful. The key is to help your nervous boss feel more comfortable and not feed his insecurities by perceiving him to be unfit as a result of his anxieties.

The Politician

The boss who is political can be a good thing if he also cares about the work and his team. This boss will work the political landscape to ensure he, his department, and his people are viewed as important to the organization's purpose. The political boss who only cares about his own status in the organization is not good. The latter has the potential to blindside you and others.

The Indecisive Boss

This boss can't and won't make a decision, likely out of fear of being wrong. She is obviously not as confident as she should be for her position, may not always be prepared (from an information perspective), may not be responsive or may put up barriers in order to avoid making decisions, and may fear taking risks. You can be helpful to this boss, provided she is not threatened by your take-charge approach. You can gather all the pertinent information and make a pro/con analysis of a particular decision that needs to be made. This may be the road map that the boss needs to see in order to facilitate the decisions that need to be made or the approach that needs to be taken.

The Pirate:

Keep your hands in your pockets. This boss type tends to steal others' ideas and puts them forth as his own. It's a survival mechanism for the boss who is afraid that his best days are behind him and who is trying to appear relevant in a changing/challenging work environment.

The Barnacle:

> She is a parasite that attaches herself to people with great ideas and loads of talent. She lives off the great works of others. She slows down the progress of others while contributing little. Sad really.

The Moron:

> Not so much low IQ as a stunted, in-the-box, very limited, by-the-book approach to thinking. It does not serve you any good purpose to act in a way that implies that you believe your boss is a moron.

The Ignoramus:

> There's a difference between stupidity and ignorance. Stupidity is outside your control while ignorance is inside your control. You can always find out things you don't know, but if you don't have the capacity to process new information, then your possibilities are limited. The Ignoramus is a leader who just refuses to acquire new information and change with the times. Again, you can be helpful to this boss by obtaining the relevant information and preparing the road map for what needs to be done.

The Hypocrite:

> A leader who says, "Do as I say, not as I do."

The Daredevil:

> The beaver that is too eager, attempting everything and achieving nothing, hoping hyperactivity compensates for lack of thoughtful reflection.

The Peacenik:

> This boss cannot permit conflict, including the healthy storming necessary to create a strong team.

The Jingo:

> This leader doesn't value diversity and wants to keep people and ideas homogenous.

The Spaceman:

> This boss is so smart that no one can fathom what she is saying.

The Softie:

> People need to be pushed occasionally, but this leader is too nice to do the pushing. It's ok to tell your boss that sometimes it's ok to be strict.

The Misfit:

> This boss simply possesses the wrong style or approach for the team at hand. You can have superior skills and talents and still be a misfit.

The Self-Server:

> This toxic leader is equally as challenging as the bad politician boss. She puts herself above the needs of others.

The Hermit:

> This boss really doesn't know the people on his team and can't overcome his or her natural reserve. The best approach with this type of boss is to take a genuine interest in

him as a person and a leader in the organization. Again, instilling trust in this type of boss that you are committed to the job and loyal to his team will go a long way.

The Vacillator:

Inconsistency and leadership don't mix. This boss changes course often. It is confusing and unsettling to the team when the boss often changes his mind on things. In this case, if the team can speak up as a unit, it may be more impactful. As a team, you can articulate that changing course frequently causes confusion and a sense that there is not a clear path to accomplishing goals and that such an approach is not ultimately beneficial for the team's success.

The Swashbuckler:

A leader who cannot take a back seat is not a "servant leader," but rather, one who has to be in "follow-me" mode all the time, creating a sense of excitement by continuous activity. Swashbucklers wear people out over time.

The Nepotist:

This leader plays favorites and consigns others to the woodshed. Do your job well and be a person others like to work with and one that your boss can rely on to get a job done.

The Blamer:

This boss is more interested in tabbing a fall guy than in learning from mistakes. If you are the fall guy and you played a role in what went wrong, own it and ask your boss if you and she can meet to discuss the lessons from the mistake.

The Alien:

This leader is oblivious to the personal/career needs of others on his team. The key to influencing the Alien boss is to communicate in a way that is informative and instructive (not threatening).

The Coward:

This boss is unwilling to fight for the needs of her team members.

The Cinder:

This boss is passive, burned-out and can no longer generate sparks in others.

The Traitor:

This leader deceives the team or sells it out. There is no recovery—ever—from the loss of trust resulting from betrayal.

Using the behavioral dimensions we identified earlier, you will have the ability to deal with difficult bosses and colleagues. Remember, there is always a strategy to be implemented with most of these types of difficult bosses. You may need objective guidance in helping you develop and implement the strategy. In our experience, those who effect a strategy often meet with success or at the least, feel very empowered to manage the situation and person at hand.

What to Do When Conflict Arises

When someone does something or doesn't do something that causes conflict for you, your immediate reaction and natural tendency may be to:

- Be angry
- Get defensive
- Tell the person off
- Shut down
- Get rebellious
- Want to quit
- Feel like getting even
- Internalize failure/self-doubt.

When dealing with difficult people, it's easy to get caught up in the emotions of the moment. Instead, try to understand your own internal reality and develop a clinical rather than an emotional response. Ask yourself: What feelings are triggered by my own life experiences? What could the triggers be for the other person's behaviors or reactions? When dealing with difficult people or a difficult situation, try to understand where they're coming from, try to read their mind. Take a deep breath and really listen and process mentally what is happening at the moment and why. Do not interrupt or try to argue your position. Repeat back what was said to you to ensure them that you understand their perspective and heard what they said. The purpose of this is to make sure that they understand that you heard what they said. You may not agree with what they said but you can acknowledge that you heard what their perspective was. This is active listening. Ask questions to clarify anything that is unclear. Continue to assess the situation without becoming emotional and try not to be judgmental. Compartmentalize the situation. If your boss or colleague is claiming you did something wrong or failed to do something, focus on the situation at hand as opposed to concluding that your entire job stinks. Ask yourself whether you want your reaction to be your first choice or last option. Remember that body language is important. Ensure that your body language connotes that you desire to resolve the problem as opposed to escalating it.

Mara's friend, Martha Seiver, worked for a major investment bank on the trading floor after having worked in a creative job for a fashion design house. Landing the job was a huge surprise to her since she went on the interview merely to practice her interview skills after her friend told her about an assistant trader position for a manager who had fired every assistant he ever had. Her first day on the job, the manager gave her this advice: "You will be fine in this position if you remember two things: be responsive and never assume." After many months of success in her new role, the manager asked her to make sure all members of the team attended an all-hands-on-deck meeting to be followed by a social event. One important member, who we will call Tom, didn't show up. The manager was furious. He called Martha into his office, screamed at her and accused her of failing to inform Tom of the meeting. Tom apparently told the manager he didn't know about the meeting. Martha respectfully pushed back and told her manager that, in fact, she did tell Tom about the meeting and described the office setting and the day when it occurred. After the heated confrontation, the manager finally said to Martha, "I'm sure you did tell Tom." From that moment on, Martha made sure that when she informed the team of an upcoming meeting, she had them acknowledge that they were so informed and had them initial a piece of paper that indicated that on that date Martha informed them of the meeting. This story has several lessons. First, practice interviews are very important – you just never know what the outcome will be. Second, active listening took place whereby Martha required the recipient of her information to acknowledge what she was telling them. Third, she learned from this experience never to assume they were listening, unlike her boss who didn't follow his own advice when he assumed Martha didn't do what she was instructed to do. Fourth, she was responsive to her boss's directives, and finally, she respectfully stood up to her boss and pushed back on *his* wrong assumption.

Adaptation:

Break down and compartmentalize the situation. Focus on resolving the problem. Discuss the cause and effect of the problem behavior and ways to deal with it. Ask questions to get information rather than just stating opinions. Remember, you can't change someone's personality, but you can adapt your reactions to it.

Step in Shoes of Another:

Understand the personality type of the other person (DISC Assessment): Driver (poor listening skills, decision maker, gets things done); Influencer (influences people by talking, sees the big picture, walk in and greet); Steadfast (loyal, trustworthy, doesn't like change, finish this before you do that, repetitive behavior); Contemplative (believes in a process, sees minute details, lives in fear of making a mistake). Different learning styles: audio, visual, kinesthetic, reader/researcher.

Drive the Outcome:

Influence his/her attitude. What do you want them to think and do? In a non-confrontational, honest, nonjudgmental, from-the-heart way, assess the situation and explain how the behavior has affected you. Explain what could have been done differently if the "redo" button could be pushed. Explore different ways to handle the situation. Engage in thinking technically and thinking psychologically.

Engage in Clinical Communication:

Speak directly and honestly and in terms of "I feel humiliated when I am being yelled at in front of my coworkers"; "I cannot meet my deadline when I do not have access to your input on the project." Do not place blame or find fault; rather, focus on positive ways that similar situations could be dealt with in order to prevent the problem from recurring in the future.

Mantras

1. ***Be calm.*** Losing your temper and lashing out at the other person typically isn't the best way to get him/her to work

with you. Unless you know that anger will trigger the person into action and you are consciously using it as a strategy to move them, it is better to assume a calm, clinical persona. Someone who is calm is seen as being in control, centered, and more respected. Most people would prefer to work with someone who is predominantly calm rather than someone who is always on edge. When the person you are dealing with sees that you are calm despite whatever he/she is doing, you will start getting their attention. The other person will see that your feathers are not being ruffled as a result of his/her high emotions, high stress level and personal attacks.

2. ***Understand the person's intentions.*** No one is difficult for the sake of being difficult. Even when it may seem that the person is vindictive, there is always some underlying motivation for them to act that way. Rarely is this motivation apparent. Try to identify the person's trigger: What is making him/her act in this manner? What is stopping him/her from cooperating with you? How can you help to meet his/her needs and resolve the situation?

3. ***Get some perspective by seeking input from others.*** In all likelihood, your colleagues and friends have experienced similar situations. They will be able to see things from a different angle and offer a different take on the situation. This has to be handled delicately because you do not want to be viewed as an antagonist or a gossiper. You have to trust the person with whom you share your story. Listen to

what they have to say. You might very well find some golden advice.

4. ***Let the person know where you are coming from.*** One thing that works is to let the person know your intentions. Sometimes, they are being resistant because they think that you are just being difficult with them, preventing them from reaching their desired end result, or that you are not with the program. Letting them in on the reason behind your actions, reservations, thinking, and the full background of what is happening may enable them to empathize with your situation and even see your perspective.

5. ***Build rapport.*** Step Ladder Approach: Establish a relationship, establish trust, see the big picture. With all the computers, emails, and messaging systems, work sometimes turns into a mechanical process. Re-instill the human touch by connecting with your colleagues on a personal level. If you have an opportunity to have a live conversation with them, pick yourself up from your desk and have a live conversation with them. Go out with them for lunches or dinners. Get to know them as people and not colleagues. Learn more about their hobbies, their family, their lives. Foster strong connections. These will go a long way in building and improving relationships in your work world.

6. ***Always treat the person with respect.*** No one likes to be treated as if he/she is stupid/incapable/incompetent. If you treat someone with disrespect, don't be surprised if he/she

treats you the same way. As the golden rule says, "Do unto others as you would have them do unto you." Don't misunderstand someone giving you direction or constructive feedback. Unfortunately, not everyone lives by this edict. When someone treats you disrespectfully, you will need to speak up in order to set boundaries for yourself. It's ok to do so even if the person is senior to you. It is the way in which you do this that is key. Speak in terms of how it feels when the person treats you that way. Express that you are willing to take criticism but you will respond better to it if it is given respectfully. When you do this, the outcome will be very surprising to you; trust us.

7.   ***Focus on what can be acted upon***. Sometimes, you may be put into a difficult situation by your difficult colleagues, such as not receiving a piece of work they promised to give or being wrongly held responsible for something you didn't or weren't supposed to do. Whatever it is, acknowledge that the situation has already occurred. Rather than harp on what you cannot change, focus on the actionable steps you can take to move forward in the situation.

8.   ***Ignore***. If you have already tried everything above and the person is still not being receptive, the best way might be to just ignore it and move on. There are bad guys in positions of authority who are destructive and taking them on could be a job ender. You have already done all that you can within your means. Get on with your daily tasks and interface with the person only where and when needed. Of

course, this isn't feasible in cases where the person plays a critical role in your work, which leads us to our last tip.

9. ***Develop an Exit Strategy.*** Your situation may be intolerable for you in light of a toxic situation and/or destructive boss. It may be time for you to look for another job. You need to do this thoughtfully and in a way that does not impede your current responsibilities. Obtaining an advisor to help you set goals, prepare for interviews, be discerning in terms of the environment you are seeking, and negotiate for terms commensurate with your level is a wise step to take.

There are two stories that come to mind to depict successful defusion of a very difficult situation caused by very difficult individuals. The lessons from these stories are significant.

Dear Lord Prayer

A very close friend of Mara's told her a story[lxv] of how she single-handedly turned a monster boss into a saint when the friend was a young trader. Here is her story.

"Wow, I'm finally entering the workforce. I am done with school, my parents have paid for my room and board for the last time (hopefully), and I am walking into a world I think I can conquer, but blindly so. I have always entered a challenge with a PMA (positive mental attitude).

Yet, my spectacles were definitely rose-colored and, in retrospect, I was not always realistic about the challenges I was about to face. This can be a good or a bad thing. Do you want to know you're falling off the cliff before you get there and be as prepared as possible or do you want to figure out what to do while you are halfway down to near death? I figured it out along the way, but definitely would have preferred to have some heads-up ahead of time.

Anyway, here I am walking into my first job on Wall Street, feeling excited but a bit unprepared after attaining this incredible first job. A bit unprepared puts it mildly; *I had no idea what I was doing.*

Make no mistake, I never let that feeling show and after many years, I came to understand that only very few college graduates know what they are doing when they walk through the working door for the first time. I entered the glamorous world of the trading desk.

Two hundred and fifty people were all sitting in close quarters, trading municipal bonds, government bonds, foreign currency, CDs, fed funds, and the like and all were trying to make money. Tensions definitely arose every now and then, as you can imagine when dealing with that many millions. I had the pleasure of sitting on the municipal bond desk or munis, as it is affectionately referred as. As a new liaison to the satellite offices in Chicago, Atlanta, LA, and Dallas, my job had just been created and I was to work closely with the short-term bond trader, an established trader who had just been acquired from a strong competitor. He was the boss, the established "good guy," and most important, the moneymaker. I was just the lowly graduate finding my way in this sea of green. Well, to say he was a hothead would not be giving this story justice. At least several times a day (and if you had asked me then, I would have said all day) he yelled at me and called me a @#*$(&$*§+@#. I felt like the most incompetent creature on the planet when he did that. Despondent and alone, I thought I would never make it there in the Big Apple and, therefore, never make it anywhere! Finally, I returned to the source, the end all and be all who knew when I was cold, when I needed to sleep, and most important, the one who thought I was brilliant on every front. Yes, I called my mom and told her all about the Big Bad Wolf.

Let me stop here and tell you a bit about my mom. She makes me look like Chicken Little when it comes to outlook. As the most positive person I know in the world, she has delivered phrases like "You are a diamond and all you have to do is find your proper setting." That was when I walked into a party to see my boyfriend kissing another girl.

"Never a door will close that another one won't open" came when I lost three out of five dance parts *the day before* the recital. Now you get a slight window into my mom's heart. But, the incredible beauty of our relationship was that I believed everything she said, hook, line, and sinker.

So, getting back to the problem at hand, I knew I was in way over my head with this Chief Trader Monster and needed words of wisdom to deal with the insurmountable problem of his abuse. And of course, once again, she delivered. She did not have a phrase in her bag of tricks; but rather, she gave me a card displaying an all-important phrase I will carry with me for the rest of my life. The card read:

"Lord, help me to remember nothing will happen to me today that you and I cannot handle together."

She simply handed me the card and told me to work it into the conversation sometime throughout the day with the Monster. Imagine that! Tell one of the hottest shots on Wall Street that I had the Lord (and my mom) on my side and he better watch out because those Higher Powers would handle him if he did not stop handling me! With my card in hand, I went to work the next day armed and ready.

Predictably, he rose from his seat about mid-morning, bright red in the face, leaned over the desk, and yelled in my face, in front of the entire trading floor, that I was an asshole for making a particular trade. No sad face this time. The moment had arrived...

Bolting out of my seat, I whipped out my card and put it directly in front of his face. Stopping dead in his tracks, he read the message while slowly sitting back in his chair. Stunned, he told me his twin brother was a Jesuit priest who wouldn't be happy with his behavior.

From that day forward, we worked very well together; I had earned the respect I deserved. Not necessarily from excelling at my position, but rather, from knowing how to work and influence a very challenging boss. I understood a few things I will never forget. One, never, never, never believe that you can't change a situation to make it work better for you. Two, always understand who you are and be creative within that framework. Success means stepping out of your comfort zone to achieve your goals. And three, Mom knows best!"

Here is Mara's story.

The Five-Hour Lunch

I received a call from an old friend and colleague from my law firm whom I had not spoken to in quite some time. I had left my firm in 2005 and it was now 2012. Sam had left my old firm in 2011 and joined a competitor firm. Sam had had one major client when he was at our old firm. I was employment counsel for that client. Sam and I worked closely together and we were friends (we grew up in the firm together). He was definitely considered a micromanager and rightly so, because he was protective of his major (only) client. Sam asked me to lunch. His call was a surprise and his invitation to lunch an even bigger surprise. I traveled to NYC for lunch with him, and we went to a restaurant near his office at around 12:30pm. We had a lot to catch up on: his decision to leave his firm, his family, my practice, my family, his big client for whom I consulted for two years after I left my firm. Sam had so much to say. People who know me often joke how much I like to talk, but Sam was a real talker, a very fast talker. He talked so much that our weekday lunch was going on multiple hours. Sam spent over an hour and a half telling me about the intricate details of his wife's back surgery and the toll her disability and recovery took on his family. He spoke about all that he had to do to hold down the family fort all while working long lawyer hours. He talked in painstaking detail about his decision to leave our firm and the process of landing a new position at a different firm. It was virtually impossible to get a word in edgewise. When I tried to, Sam would say, "Just let me finish ..." We left the restaurant at 4:30pm. We had sat at lunch for four hours. In lawyer terms, let me tell you what this means. Sam bills out at somewhere around $800/hour, and I bill out at $300. In total, we lost $4,400 in productivity and billables sitting in the restaurant at lunch, eating and talking. That wasn't where it ended. Sam asked me back to his office, where he talked until 5:15pm. I finally told him that I had to leave to catch a train. It was astounding that we had had a five-hour lunch that afternoon from when we said hello to good-bye. A total of $6,050 in lost productivity. It was even more astounding that Sam could talk for that long. The next day I was in my office and the phone rang. A NYC number popped up and when I answered ... I panicked. It was Sam. I could not imagine losing another day's worth of business.

The conversation went like this:

Sam: "Hi, Mara. I had a question for you. I was thinking about our lunch yesterday. I would like to give you some feedback. Did anyone ever give you feedback that you talk too much? I get that feedback, too, sometimes and I just wanted to give you that feedback."

Mara's Thought Process: I was shocked. The anger started in my toes and rose up my body in a nanosecond. I thought, "How dare he …" He talked for over five hours and is accusing me of talking too much. In a split second, I processed what he said to me. I took a deep breath. Here is what I said to him, despite my emotional instinct to want to reach into the phone and rip his lungs out.

Mara: "Sam, I know that we talked for over five hours. In lawyer time, that's a lot of potential billable hours not billed by either of us. That said, we haven't seen each other in five years so if you amortize that five-hour lunch over the five years we haven't seen each other, it is as if we had lunch each year for only an hour. We obviously had a lot of business, personal, and family subject matter to cover. I think that you should just chalk it up to two friends catching up and not worry that we spent an afternoon doing that."

He agreed and we both said it was great catching up and seeing each other. We wished each other well and sent regards to our respective families.

Mara defused the situation despite feeling so angry. She, within an instant, stepped into Sam's shoes and wondered what on earth he must have been thinking. She gathered that he was feeling guilty about spending so much time out of the office on non-billable stuff. It was easy for him to project his disagreeable character trait onto Mara, and she had a few options: (a) she could have attacked and asked him what the #$*&?; (b) she could have been defensive and said "Me? You talked to me about your wife's back surgery for an hour and a half and then you talked to me about leaving our firm for another hour and a half and your boys for another two hours;" or (c) she could have answered in a way that showed him that he was not going to get a rise out of her, that she knew the truth of what transpired, and that it would be nothing for her to defuse the situation because she was so "comfortable in her own skin." She chose the latter response.

"Psychological projection is a theory in psychology that says that humans defend themselves against unpleasant impulses by denying their existence in themselves, while attributing them to others. For example, a person who is rude may constantly accuse other people of being rude. According to some research, the projection of one's negative qualities onto others is a common process in everyday life."[lxvi]

Versatility

We talked about this behavioral dimension in Part I. The key to successful versatility is to answer the question, "Who's responsible for what, by when, and how are we going to check with each other to make sure we're on track or modify our path depending on the circumstances." To do what you need to, make sure that in every conversation you have with others you include the What (to appeal to the Driver), the Why (to appeal to the Expressive), the How (to appeal to the Analytical), and the Who (to appeal to the Amiable). This may not be your typical way of responding to others but if you do, you will demonstrate the versatility needed to deal with all kinds of people. For example, you are in a meeting to discuss the new project everyone is anxious to hear about:

You say:　　"Based on our most recent customer surveys that included 15,000 people answering both in-store and online questionnaires about our service, we have decided to increase our customer's positive experience by allowing our cashiers to negotiate the price of any product in dispute at the checkout counter rather than calling back to the department and doing a price check, which delays checkout. Our plan is to train all of our cashiers on the new procedure over the next three months and discuss the range within which they can negotiate with the customer at checkout. This project will formally start with a kick-off meeting led by each store manager once all cashiers have completed the training. Our hope is that this new policy will result in an increase in sales per customer and more frequent customer store visits, with more customers making inquiries with our trained sales force thus increasing our profits."

George: "Why are we implementing this new process now?

You: "We want this new procedure up and running before the next busy holiday season since we anticipate an increase in customer traffic at that time. This new process should smooth out many of the delays related to unmarked store items or differences between what is marked on the item and any special pricing that is indicated on the shelf."

Nancy: "How did you make the decision to survey the customers? Was something wrong with what we were doing before?"

You: "Well, Nancy, as you know, we continuously monitor what our customers are asking for to determine ways to improve their in-store experience. When we learned from customer comments that some were unsure who to ask for in-store help, we got new T-shirts that said ASK ME on the back.

As you can see from this dialogue, it is important to answer the *How, What, Why,* and *Who* questions in every conversation to make sure that you are unlocking the minds (increasing the reception) of the four main personality traits we've discussed; Driver, Expressive, Analytical, and Amiable.

3D Versatility

We've talked about the four personality styles that leaders can exhibit: Driver, Expressive, Amiable, and Analytical. That's pretty straightforward—we can all pick out people around us who have these traits. But, there's a dimension that can be added to these styles that adds just a touch of interest and creates a 3D model of versatility. It's called *Introversion/Extraversion.*

You may naturally think of an Analytical person as being basically introverted. It's also possible to have an extroverted Analytical—someone who will chase you down the hallway shouting rules and regulations, making demands on your time and commitments to following the established policies and procedures. An introverted Analytical will sit at her desk all day writing policies and procedures, getting deep vein thrombosis. But, when they leave the office, their desks are so clean it's as if they were never there.

It's also possible to have an introverted Expressive, someone who walks down the hall with a twinkle in his/her eye, whistling tunes, smiling. In their minds, they're having a party. They're just not sharing it with anyone. Extroverted Expressives talk a lot, engage others in their conversations, and start work groups to create new practices. They are Intrepreneurs (Entrepreneurs within the company).

While you may think of Drivers as being extroverted by nature, you can also have an introverted Driver. This is someone who drives themselves rather than others and holds themselves to unreasonably high standards. They will do anything to not make mistakes. Extroverted Drivers are the ones standing at the helm shouting orders to their followers and keeping people focused on the outcomes of the group.

And you can have an introverted Amiable. These people are continuously in the mode of self-improvement. They have a calm sense of self. Their face is not contorted with the stresses of the day. They go for walks over lunch, eat nuts, grasses, drink green tea, and sit cross-legged on their desk balls. The extroverted Amiable is the person who intentionally builds bridges between departments, fosters communication and teamwork, starts common interest work groups, posts successful team outcomes in internal newsletters, and touches your arm when speaking to you.

It is well documented that people who understand differences in communication preferences and learn to adapt their own communications to make others more comfortable are more effective leaders. Employees don't leave companies; they leave managers. Numerous studies have shown that the most common reason people give for leaving a job is a poor relationship with their manager. Turnover, productivity, performance, and employee satisfaction are all tied to a manager's ability to build effective relationships with employees. Versatility is the key. Several studies in the past have shown the link between performance measures and versatility scores as well as how versatility actually works in the manager-employee relationship. A leader who is sensitive to the style of his or her employees, and takes steps to adjust his or her behavior to meet the needs of others, will communicate more clearly and establish a more trusting relationship.[lxvii]

Chapter 7

Leadership: Batten Down

As you enter and move up in your organization, you need to understand a few truths about human nature and the art of followership as well as leadership. Each young adult aspiring to be a leader in his or her field and organization must learn the qualities and skills of a leader even in the absence of an actual title or designation. This chapter provides tips for your development as a leader. Some of our teachings below assume that you have come into a leadership role or are being groomed for one.

Overcome Fear

Everyone's afraid. People are afraid of failure and of looking bad in the eyes of others. People are afraid of not being as smart as they want to appear. And, as we have learned, young people fear making mistakes. It really doesn't matter whether you are at the bottom of the totem pole trying to find your way or are currently in a leadership role. People are people and behave in quite predictable ways. Take for example, the young adult who wants to respect the time of his boss. As a result, she doesn't want to bother the boss with what she may think are non-issues (things that don't seem important). So she doesn't tell the boss what's going on, thinking she can handle it on her own. Surprise, surprise, the boss is upset. It's not that she doesn't show initiative, it's the fact that the boss is afraid of not knowing what's going on and by not communicating with the boss, she has played right into the boss's fears. Someone above that boss may ask him a question for which he may not know the answer. So, he gets in her business and micromanages her. Fear. To avoid this micromanagement, you need to over-communicate with your boss. Give the boss more, not less, information. You can always tell the boss what the issue is, what you think you should do about it, and ask for his permission to proceed. That way, you show your value, and reduce your boss's fear of not knowing what's up.

Leaders are often afraid that they don't have the skills necessary to fulfill the requirements of their job. There is always the concern that they will be found out as frauds. No one has all that they need to succeed on their own without the input and assistance of others. Great leaders know that. New or aspiring leaders often don't know that. These new leaders often feel that they were promoted for being good at their jobs, for being smart. The good news is that young adults, in general, are collaborative by nature. To succeed in any position, hold on to your desire to collaborate and learn from others.

Engage with Colleagues

In terms of followers (and everyone in organizations reports to someone), it's important to be engaged. Quite often people new to organizations try to stay out of sight. They hide. They don't want to stand out so that they won't get criticized. Get used to criticism. Ask for it. Learn from it. Use it to learn and become better. Show others that you've learned and are determined to continue to learn and you'll become valuable. Follow orders. Make suggestions to improve the orders of others. Do not stray from the task or job you've been given without the knowledge and approval of your boss. If you must, tell them what you are going to do and when (in a few days or week) and tell them (in an email) that you will initiate action unless you hear from them to either stop or to modify your trajectory (this is called a broadcast letter). If you don't hear back from them, go for it. Just make sure to keep them informed of your progress at every step in the process. When you're done—and hopefully successful—give the boss a good chunk of the credit.

Share your Passion

The people above you in the chain of command are often intimidated and threatened by young adults. Why? Because you've got something they do not have or have lost but would love to regain. You've got passion, smarts, confidence, and an intimate connection to technology. They're jealous (want it for themselves and do not want you to have it) or if they are really good souls, merely envious (simply want it for themselves, too). Don't scare them. Collaborate with them. Bring them into your circle. Help them help you. One of these days, when the next generation enters the workforce, you will be the scared ones because they will inevitably bring something to the workforce that you don't have. Create a better future for yourself by creating a better, more collaborative, informative environment now that includes your boss in the equation. Make them want to be your mentors. They may kick and scream because, as we said before, they are afraid and jealous (or envious) of your potential and your confidence. You can and should make them better leaders by being better followers.

Oh Captain, My Captain:
What Young Adult Leaders Must Do

Create internal motivation in others. I can see it now. The Boomer boss shouting orders to the crew, line in one hand, saber in the other. "Come on, mates," he shouts, swinging through the office as if from yardarm to yardarm. The young crewmate looks up and mutters, "'scuse me?"

Young adults have far different expectations of their leaders than prior generations had of their bosses. To gain the respect of all generations, there are some basic requirements that young adult (potential) leaders must learn to master. But what does it take to motivate others? Well, we hate to bust your bubble, but you don't have what it takes to motivate others. No one does. It's a fool's journey. Motivation is an internal force, not some external goop that you can spray around the office like Febreze.

It's human nature. People are motivated by the successful completion of short-term, high-priority goals and objectives. Make to-do lists. By creating an environment of short-term, high-priority targets, you create internal motivation in others as they check the items at the top of the list off as they get completed. They can't wait to come into work the next day and take aim at the next item on the list.

Develop Autonomy

People want to be self-directed, to have control over their lives and destinies. To the extent that we don't have autonomy, we feel something is missing.

Develop Mastery

People want to get better at things. We need to learn to master the tasks we are undertaking.

Be Purposeful

Make the world a little bit better. We need buy-in as to why we are doing things. There needs to be a reason.

What motivates human beings, at least at work, is the successful completion of clearly defined, high-priority goals and objectives. Just take a look at the honey-do lists that you (or your significant other) create. You do the things at the top of the list, not because you are hounded to do them (mostly), but because it feels good when you're done and you physically cross the item off the list. Sounds simple, right? But, it's not.

Back in 1968, Dr. Fred Herzberg (a motivational expert) came up with a theory he called the Motivation/Hygiene theory. He said that what most people think of as motivating is really not: pay, a nice working environment, free Mountain Dew, and a gym to work off the stresses of the day. These things may be what people want, but they don't motivate anyone to do better. They are what people expect to have; Herzberg labeled them *hygiene* factors. If you provide them, people will be happy because you met their expectations. But you won't motivate them. However, if you don't provide these expectations, you might demotivate people.

So, what motivates others, makes them want to follow you as their leader? Providing clear and consistent high-priority goals tied to the goals of the overall company, your team honey-do list.

Take all of your goals/objectives and sort them into timeframes: short term, midterm, and long term. Short term goals are things that need to be accomplished within the next thirty days. Midterm goals are those things that need to be done within one to three months. Long-term goals are things that need to be done between three and six months out. You can also create a category for those goals beyond six months. Then you prioritize only the short term list: high priorities and low priorities. Don't prioritize the other categories.

As things get done, cross them off the list. As time passes, some of the midterm goals become short term and are added to the short-term list, and the short term list is then reprioritized. You reprioritize this short term list every thirty days or less.

Then you identify the goals that seem to remain at the bottom of the list after each reprioritization. We'll call them bilge; you know, the crap at the bottom of the boat that no one wants. Get rid of them: delegate them elsewhere or tag them with very long timeframes.

Be Open, Fair, and Willing to Listen

We realize that for most of you, fairness is an important issue, both for yourself and others. You need to *show* others, however, that fairness is important to you by telling people that you want to be fair. Then they will look at your behaviors to see if they are consistent with your desire to be fair. If you say one thing and do another, you will be labeled as one of bad leaders outlined above. You need to also let them know that if things don't seem fair to them, you are open and willing to listen to their concerns.

Be Decisive

It is better to make a bad decision than no decision at all. If you are seen as indecisive, people will not trust you and not view you as a team player and/or leader. The good news is that you don't have to be perfect. Use your best judgment and head in a direction. If you make a mistake, people will forgive you if you apologize and offer to redo or correct the mistake. Then head off in another direction again. People will follow. Just don't screw up too often.

Support All Team Members

If you have siblings, you know what it's like. You fight, call names ... then make up. It's OK to beat up on your family members, but it's not OK if others try to beat up on them. You protect your family from others with ill intent. Same goes for your team. It's OK to beat up on your team members, but it's not OK to allow others to do the same. You protect your team members even if you have your own personal disputes with them. They are your family.

Take Responsibility for Bad Outcomes

If your boat runs aground, take responsibility for the bad outcome. Don't do what a friend of ours calls "blamestorming"—looking for someone at whom to point the finger. Whether you had anything to do with the bad outcomes, you take personal responsibility if you are the leader. It's hard; especially when you know others were at fault. The quickest way to tear the fabric of a team apart is to look for scapegoats.

Give Credit to Team Members

When the team wins, everyone wins. This is not a new concept for young adults to understand. However, you are in the boat with others who don't necessarily share your altruistic view of the world. Many want to take the credit for positive outcomes and expect to receive the praise they think they deserve, especially in a competitive environment. What good leaders do, however, is share the credit and praise evenly among all team members. You win (and lose) together as a team. Great leaders not only give the team credit, but additionally shine a light on the individuals who helped the team win the most. So, in essence, it's a single lose (everyone loses together), dual win (both the team and specific individuals win) environment that you create.

Be Sensitive to Team Members

This deals with two types of sensitivity. People who work for a leader do not normally put forth their best efforts unless they get some recognition of their needs and are provided with the flexibility (if possible) to meet those needs. It could be some brief time off to deal with a personal issue. Or it could be the ability to work with/contribute to a different group for a while in order to pick up a new skill not needed in the current job.

The second area of sensitivity, which we believe is more important, is what we call "little missiles." You know, the quips you shoot at each other for fun. "Hey Jamie, nice job the other day. It's about time you used your head for more than a hat rack." This may be funny for you but not for the other person. We shoot these little missiles at each other with impunity to the point where we don't even think about it and wonder why the other person doesn't get the joke.

Well, you know when you are about to pull the trigger. Be mindful of your intentions and the potential reactions from your targets (you don't know what's on their minds at the time you send a missile their way), and don't pull the trigger.

Respect the Opinions of Others

Many years ago, as an undergraduate, Harvey was in a class known for being filled with brilliant people. They were all told they were brilliant, and they believed it wholeheartedly. For nearly all the problems presented, the students usually had the same answers. They thought they were God's gift. Then one day, the professor walks in and hands out an assignment. The piece of paper handed out was titled: The Problem. They were told to go home (no class today), figure out the solution, and be prepared to present their solution the next day. Easy peasy. The professor even handed out a separate piece of paper with additional information on it to each person as they walked out of the room.

The next day everyone compared the problems they had been given. As each had the exact same problem, they thought, no sweat. They imagined that since they were obviously all brilliant, they'd all have the same solution to the problem.

Once the first person stood up to present, the students, including Harvey, all realized that they were in for some major conflict. The first person's solution was nothing like what Harvey was about to present as his solution. The muttering in the room indicated to him that he was not the only one in disagreement with what was being presented. After a few of the students had presented, the name-calling started. "What are you thinking?" "Are you serious?" "That's the dumbest thing I've ever heard." "That won't work!" "You're an idiot." Tempers started to flare until the professor stepped in and asked what the problem was. They all chimed in and said that they had the correct answer and that everyone else was wrong. Then he asked how the students had gone about solving the problem, and they referenced the additional piece of paper they were given the day before. At that point, the professor stated they were all idiots, enamored with their own brilliance. The additional piece of paper provided different information to each of them, background information that supposedly created the problem.

Then he said, "The next time you think you have the correct answer, ask yourself, 'what's the second right answer?' because everyone is operating from different scripts. Be open to the opinions of others. It will make you better people." Silence filled the room. Everyone felt humbled … and enriched.

The next time you are enamored with your brilliance because your parents/teachers told you so, ask yourself the question, "what's the second right answer?" and go find others' opinions/inputs. It will not only make your output more brilliant, but it will also send a message to others that you value their input.

Empower Others to Act

People want the responsibility of accomplishing something meaningful. It is where motivation comes from. So how do you do that in a way that prevents you from continuously coming back to your superiors, seeking their advice/input, and stealing their time? If you are that superior, how do you prevent others from doing the same to you?

Let's face it, as we said before, people are afraid of making mistakes and making decisions that will be questioned later. They just don't know where their decision-making boundaries are because no one told them what they were. They haven't been enabled to pick up the ball and run with it (empowered to make independent decisions). To get this from your boss, sit down with her and ask for guidelines around such things as resources, quantity, quality, and timeframes. You need to know how much leeway, if any, you have, and when you must get your boss's input. If you are the boss, let each individual know (based on their skill level and experience) the limits within which they are free to make independent decisions (while keeping you in the information loop). At what point do you want them to come to you? Of course, this doesn't guarantee independent decisions will be made, but if you lay the groundwork, you can catch your subordinates doing what you asked and reward them for their ambitious efforts. Your boss may do the same for you.

Set the Direction

People need to know where the company and their business unit are heading. A company's vision states what they stand for, what they want to be known for. How they get there should be reflected in the mission statement(s). It is your responsibility as a new leader to translate the bigger, broader company vision and mission into your own business unit's vision and mission. You must align your smaller mission with the mission of the larger organization and then look around to make sure that what your business unit does is not in conflict with the mission of other business units with which you must coordinate. Use your natural preference to collaborate/coordinate with other like-minded people in other business units to make a cohesive force. Your specific goals and individual roles/responsibilities flow from the mission statements you create in collaboration with the people in your business unit and other business divisions within the organization.

Values are really behavioral expectations. You have group discussions in which you agree on how you will behave toward each other, how you will resolve disagreements and make decisions, and who you will coordinate with to achieve the outcomes you need.

Set Some Goals

This is where all good leadership begins. As mentioned above, all goals flow from your mission statement(s) and should be prioritized into short-, mid-, and long-term goals for maximum impact. Without a timeframe for goal completion, you are dealing with dreams and desires, and you are not grounded in the world of reality. No timeframe, no goal.

Define Some Roles

One of the most critical questions that a leader can ask is, "Who is responsible for what, by when, and how are we going to check with each other to make sure we're on track?" Every member of your team needs to know what needs to be done to accomplish the outcomes, who will be held responsible for completing each task, who will they need input from, and how will they coordinate with those who will use their completed tasks to complete their own work. Keep in mind that, even though you may act this way, not everyone on your team will. Keeping people focused on fulfilling their agreed-upon roles toward the completion of outcomes will meet everyone's needs regardless of the generation of which they are a part.

Form Some Teams, But Not Too Many

Avoid the trap of having everything done via teams. Young adults, in general, are great team players. You've grown up doing nearly everything in teams because of the electronic ease of staying in continuous touch with those around you. Although enterprise-wide initiatives are best accomplished via teams, some of the smaller projects really need people to pull their individual weight. Not only can you have very small teams of two or three, but you can also have "teams" of one; an individual completes a task solo, keeping in mind where that task fits into the overall scheme of things for the bigger business unit. So form teams where it makes sense and avoid the temptation to create a team tyranny feeling where everyone has to belong on a team or they are cut adrift.

Give/Get Feedback

Once you set goals and create timetables for the completion of these goals, you also need to set checkpoints along the way so you can give people feedback about where things are and how they're doing. Good managers catch people doing things wrong and correct them, while good leaders catch people doing things right and reward them. Setting up checkpoints allows you the opportunity to do both. Remember, people need/want feedback. No one is comfortable feeling adrift.

To be seen as a good leader, you not only have to give people feedback, you need to ask others for feedback on how you're doing and what they want from you—and act on it. There was a popular mayor in New York City by the name of Ed Koch. He was popular for a while … until he wasn't. He ran on a campaign called "How'm I doin'?" He'd walk around the streets and ask citizens, "How'm I doin'?" He'd ask the same question at the end of any meetings he held. He even had a sign on the wall behind his desk that read, "How'm I doin'?" One day, there he was on the front cover of the NY Post walking down the steps of city hall carrying that sign under his arm, having just been voted out of office. Listening to feedback is not enough. Acting on feedback is required to gain/retain the trust of others.

Be Consistent

We all have differing strengths and weaknesses based partially on our personalities. There are times when people take on the mantle of leadership and feel that they have to behave differently today than they did yesterday; they were nice yesterday but once the captain's hat is on the person's head, they start barking orders.

Leadership is not based on any single personality type; to become more leader-like means doing whatever you deem important (taking into account the advice we are giving you). As a leader, you need to be able to deal with all types, to shift your communication style to meet the needs of others, to become more versatile. This versatility will determine whether people will trust you long term. Be consistent and resist the pull to make yourself into something that you are not. You can be a great leader no matter what your personality type is. Likewise, you can be a terrible leader even if you are a nice person. We recommend reading Adam Bryant's *Corner Office* column every week. It is on the second page of the *New York Times* Sunday Business Section. Each week a different CEO is interviewed about leadership and management. The insights you will gain from reading this column each week are immeasurable.

Create a Culture of Productivity

There are four types of cultures that a leader can create: Pummel, Push, Pull, and Pamper. They are pretty consistent with the personality type of the leader.

The Pummel culture is one of tension, stress, and turmoil. It is created by the leader (Captain Bly?) who says, "My way or the highway; no input or backtalk or disagreements allowed." If you disagree with the leader, you've just earned a one-way ticket to walk the plank. The Push culture is just as stressful as the Pummel culture with one big exception— the Push culture focuses on causing distress. The boss gets people to act by providing negative information about all the ways the organization can fail. It focuses on competition, who is taking the food off of your table. The boss lets the facts create the tension—"It wasn't me; all I did was tell you the situation." The Pull culture is one that is driven by a vision of the future coupled with a step-by-step road map to get there. While it is inspirational, it is ineffective without a logical plan. The Pamper culture is one where people are not held accountable for outcomes. Just breathing and taking up space is good enough.

The best leaders are able to create a combined Push-Pull culture, one in which they use facts and situational awareness to scare the hell out of everyone, then offer a way out of the fire by providing a road map to a future/better state. This is a great method for making change initiatives work within your organization.

Spread Some Joy

It doesn't take that much to motivate others since, as we discussed, motivation is self-generated. However, once tasks are completed, people need to feel that their efforts/outcomes are appreciated not just by peers, but by the leader. Appreciation carries a bit more heft. While motivation is self-generated, you can inspire others. Inspiration is defined as something that makes someone want to do something or that gives someone an idea about what to do or create; the power of moving the intellect and/or emotions. If you possess enthusiasm, work hard, set appropriate boundaries, and hold others accountable while at the same time exhibiting kindness and understanding and taking a genuine interest in others' well-being and success, you can inspire others to act in the fashion you want them to act.

Bring in some sandwiches to celebrate the completion of a significant task, go out for a group lunch. Write them a handwritten thank-you note (an email would be fine, too) detailing what they did and how it positively impacted the reputation of the team. Then follow up with a note sent to HR to be included in their personnel file, with a copy to them. A little recognition goes a long way.

Get a Life

Work/life balance. Young adults, in particular, have learned this lesson well. You've grown up in a world that promotes the value of maintaining your sanity in a stressful world. Others, however, may not be so enlightened. You need to keep an eye out for those who seem on the edge of becoming unglued. This is becoming more important than ever. Even when someone feels that it can't get any worse given their work situation, they need to know that resources are available to help them through the tough times. You may need to help them keep some perspective on the tradeoff between their well-being and the job. A person's well-being always trumps the job. As a leader, you may be called upon to give a person a shoulder to lean on or a kind word of encouragement. Not everyone knows how to ask for help when stressed. You can help by reaching out and sharing your philosophy of self-knowledge. Research indicates that people feel less stressed when talking about difficult issues when they are walking with each other side-by-side rather than facing each other in a tense conversation.

Get Help

Any good leader knows that you can't lead alone. This is a lesson that all generations can learn from young adults today. The Millennial generation is the most collaborative generation to date, most likely because you grew up encased in an envelope of electronics, continuous communication, and teamwork. As leaders, you need to let others know about the benefits of connecting. The Boomers were raised in an individualized, competitive world and feel that their individual achievements ought to be recognized above team outcomes. Young people have swung the pendulum in the other direction. An effective leader will encourage people to seek the input and advice of others, while also recognizing the need for individual accomplishments.

For young adults, competency rules. It doesn't really matter how long someone's been on the job or with the company. You need to identify what skills you should demonstrate in order to gain the respect of those around you *at all levels*.

Chapter 8

All Aboard: Teamwork and Collaboration

Roles

Who's responsible for what, by when, and how are you going to check with each other to make sure you're on track? Every good team leader has this phrase tattooed to their forehead ... well, taped to their desk at least. Everyone on the team needs to know who is being held accountable for the successful completion of each specific goal, when it needs to be completed, who is going to be involved in helping the person responsible, and how often the team will check to see if the goals are on track. This information needs to be updated at least every thirty days or so to prevent goal creep (you keep getting ever-so-slightly off target until you miss the goal by a mile when time's up). People change roles, other people are brought onto the team, new goals are dropped into your current mix, requiring a shuffling of roles. Lots can and will go wrong along the way, so continuously checking on roles/responsibilities is critical to team success.

Barrier Identification

There are three types of barriers/hurdles that may hamper your ability to get things done: People, Processes, and Structures.

People Barriers. Is there a jerk in the way somewhere? Many of us can identify someone we think is a jerk, right? In reality, there are fewer jerks out there relative to the population as a whole. About 70 % of the population is considered "normal." The other 30% are still not totally crazy, just a bit off bubble (transient neurosis) though not harmful to themselves or others. About 5% of this smaller 30% group, however, is, in fact, psychotic (loss of contact with reality; borderline personality-pervasive pattern of instability in interpersonal relationships, self-image, and emotions). They used to be locked away, but as facilities for the mentally ill have closed, their residents have been turned loose, and they could be working for companies like yours. They need to be identified and dealt with or removed quickly from your organization, although that is not what often happens. They remain in positions of leadership and continue to make others' lives difficult, to say the least. Most jerks don't know they are engaging in bad behavior. It is a natural tendency to avoid confronting someone who engages in nasty, bullying behavior out of fear that such confrontation will spur them onto greater bullying antics. Remember the Dear Lord story as an example of how to confront a boss who is the office jerk. If you are in a position of leadership, people are looking to you to handle this type of situation. The longer you keep some miscreant on staff, the more your credibility sinks, and people's trust in your leadership judgment will disappear. When that kind of person is your boss, we advise that you seek guidance in dealing with him and in developing an exit strategy because, in all likelihood, there is no way to influence that kind of individual.

Process Barriers. Process Barriers are those policies and procedures that may have been relevant/important at one time, but have now morphed into a massive black hole that needs to be avoided at all costs. As times change, few policies and procedures are updated. As a result, they become barriers to success that people have to work around. In good teams, these outdated policies/procedures are either tossed out the window or reworked to make them current and relevant. The responsibility for updating these outdated policies/procedures does not lie with the HR department, but with the operations folks who actually have to implement the policies.

Structural Barriers. Most organizations work in some sort of top-down triangle. Young adults like to work in circles, reporting to and working with whomever they feel they need to in order to get the results they want. They also do not like hierarchies—young adults believe that all men and women are created equal in the workplace. Intergenerational working groups can create a potential problem when Boomers want to go "up the chain of command" while young adults may not see the need. On many manufacturing floors and in many start-up companies, flat leadership models (where everyone on the team is collectively responsible for the outcome) often take precedence over hierarchical structures.

Infrastructure Supports

When looking at long-term team health, there are four masts that provide the strength and stamina driving your ship forward. They are informal feedback, team membership, team leadership, and continuous communication.

>*Informal Feedback.* Forget about the formal feedback that takes place once or twice a year, the one where forms need to be filled out and where you stare blankly at an empty box on your self-evaluation where you are supposed to fill in what makes you great or what you want to own up to as major screw-ups. Or where you have to think of what to put into the box as feedback to someone else whose behaviors you have not observed. After all, everyone's above average, right? Those formal feedback systems, while good in intention and required for HR purposes, are so poorly explained and inadequately trained, that they are often not used as designed. A pity really.
>
>A savior to the system, however, is the informal feedback mechanism. This is where people on the team give each other regular, casual feedback around issues like "what I want more of from you," "what I want less of from you," "what I want you to keep doing the same," and "what you have done really great lately." Essentially, it's about telling people what they are doing well and what needs improvement and letting them know how much you appreciate their support.

Team Membership. There are two types of team members: core team members and resource team members. Core team members are at the center of the action. They are at every team meeting, involved in every team decision. They are a small group of folks. Resource team members are a much larger group. They don't have to attend every meeting or be directly involved in every team decision. They are on call to input their advice and assistance if needed to help the team succeed. Many people want to be on a team primarily so they have access to the flow of information. That information can be shared via mass emails but does not require fifty people to be crammed into a small conference room for fear of being left out of the communication loop. There are some people, like engineers, who would automatically be assigned the role of resource team member because of their ability/need to help out many teams, not just one. So, when you are in a position to create teams, make sure you assign core and resource team roles.

Team Leadership. The leadership model you operate under should regularly be up for review in order to keep your leadership sharp and on track. Do you want a standard leadership model where one person is in charge? Do you want to have a co-leadership model because one of the leaders travels a lot and you don't want to slow down decision-making? Do you want to rotate the leadership role among several team members—probably on a cross-functional team—where the leader is the one whose function is at the center of activity at the current time? The idea is to keep leadership quick and nimble and adaptable to the situation at hand.

Communication. The idea is to keep lines of communication open between levels and functions within the organization. If you have some form of internal newsletter, have a column dedicated to project successes where you can boast about what you and others did and how you did it. Other people will learn from your successes.

Fathom This – Venturing into Deep Waters

Like we said before, it is important to have a strategy for your short-term and long-term career goals. Creating a career action plan is a good idea. This plan should be a work in progress throughout your career. For example, Part I could be entitled "my first job." Each part of the plan should set forth your long-term goals and short-term objectives to ensure that you are on track for that job. Here are some guidelines for your career action plan.

Know your depth; don't get in over your head

Your upbringing and education encouraged you to believe in yourself and to focus on your strengths. But while we know that you are definitely smart, electronically connected and adept, we also know that everyone could use more self-awareness and more maturity. The term fathom comes from the use of a line used to tell the depth of the water under your boat. A knot was tied every six feet with a weight at the end; one fathom would equal the six-foot distance between the knots. When entering uncertain waters, the captain would have a crewmember throw the line overboard and count the number of knots under water and thus the depth in fathoms. How many fathoms do you have? How deep are your knowledge, skills, and abilities? What characteristics do you possess or can you acquire to strengthen your hull if you run aground? When entering uncertain waters, the more fathoms you have under you, the better.

Process checkpoints

Back in the day, there was only one accurate way to figure out where you were on the ocean relative to where you wanted to be on the map. You would use a sextant, a chronometer, and a book of tables to calculate your latitude and longitude based on the angle of the sun or the stars and the time of day. It was easier if you were close to land, with visible landmarks or islands. Nowadays, with crowded waters, marker buoys trace a path for boats to follow to avoid trouble spots and to ensure safe passage to the final destination.

When you start on your career journey, whether it is a short, goal-oriented project or a long-term career adventure, knowing where you are and where you are heading is critical to maintaining your sanity. We've talked about this before. If you are the leader or a member of a project team, for example, not only do you need to know what your outcome is—where you are heading—but also your team members' progress toward that outcome. You can't just let the team wander off course and hope for the best. That's where progress checkpoints come in handy. They keep you and your team on track and they prevent you from deviating and wasting time. You set the goal, set the time frame for achieving that goal, and then establish several checkpoints along the way—marker buoys if you will—where you state what you expect to see at that point so that you can compare this with what you are actually seeing. If the two match, you're on target to reach your goal. If they are not the same, you need to ask what needs to be done to get back on track so you and your team can reach the next marker buoy on time.

Setting the pace – time management (the coxswain [pronounced cox'n])

No one likes to be controlled or ordered what to do. As a matter of fact, there is a condition called ODD (obstinate disobedient disorder) that is usually found in children where they defy all attempts at control and direction. Most humans grow out of it in their late teens/early twenties, but some maintain this disorder throughout their adult lives. You know them. You can say the sky is blue, yet because you said it, they will insist it's orange.

It's hard if you're in a leadership position to keep all the different personalities in your business unit heading in the same direction without a coxswain. The coxswain is the person who sits at the back of the rowboat yelling orders through a megaphone at the people with the oars. "Stroke

... Stroke ... Stroke!!!" Nowadays, it's done through a microphone. The coxswain sets the pace: how fast will you get to the marker buoys, to the finish line. They might say, "Pick up the pace," "Pull harder," or "Save your energy for the final push." Without someone making sure the business units' efforts are coordinated and in sync, it becomes an exercise in herding cats: people going at different paces in different directions, bumping into each other, stealing each other's resources, applying different strategies, and setting different priorities. You wonder who's running the place. To avoid this chaos, decide who is to be assigned the coxswain duties on your team or in your business unit. It could be one person, or you could rotate the role between different team members over time.

Where You Are and Where You're Heading

If you don't know where you're going, any destination will do. Without a map, you and your team will wander aimlessly, treading water, running in place. Ken Blanchard once instructed Harvey to take a sheet of paper and draw a line down the middle. On one side he was to write down all his goals, on the other, his schedule of that day's appointments/meetings. Ken had him compare the two sides. Then Ken told him that if one (or any) of the meetings was not directly related to the completion of a goal on the other side of the sheet, then "don't go 'cause you're wasting your time." Harvey has implemented that advice for years now and it has kept him on track and reduced the amount of wasted time devoted to completing goals/objectives.

Have a map

Know where the barriers are. Know where the end point is. Know where the safe harbors are. Know where the monsters are. Know where the enemy's missiles are located so you can steer clear. Know where your colleagues' missiles are so you can gain cover, if necessary.

Organizational savvy

While having a destination in mind and a map to get there are critical, you need someone to take the helm. Not necessarily the leader (although it often is) but the navigator or pilot. This is the person who understands the organization's politics and how to maneuver through the barriers and influence others. They know the capability of the team, and how to steer when resistance tries to keep them from moving forward. The key to being a great navigator is knowing how to tack. As we have explored elsewhere in this book, there are quite a few headwinds that can prevent you from successfully completing your goals or objectives. One of the biggest headwinds is the politics that exist in every organization where the needs of the individual compete with the priorities of the company. Young adults are often frustrated when they enter an organization with an enthusiasm to do the right thing and get things done, only to be confronted with obstacles that don't make any sense. Become a navigator. Know how to tack into the wind. Find your allies. Find your support. Get things done. Build your reputation. Reach out to people who can help you get things done. Become valuable.

Make yourself valuable

Around 1800, Napoleon I, Emperor of France, was quoted as saying, "An army marches on its stomach." What this phrase means is that you can't fight if you are hungry. On sailing ships (ancient and modern) as well as on the land ships (Conestoga wagons) of the old West, the most important person on board, second only to the captain, was the cook. Not just because he kept the crews fed, but because he was a jack-of-all-trades. When the surgeon was busy—or non-existent—he would do the sewing of skin and cloth. Everyone protected, supported, and (while giving him grief) loved the cook. Why? The cook was indispensable. Life was much better with the cook on board than without him. Not that you should learn to roast a pig or toss a salad, but you should learn to be as indispensable as you can be (recognizing and fully understanding, of course, that, from any organization's perspective, no one is indispensable). Make it hard for people to live without your input, support, advice, and assistance. Do your research, know your material, share information, and volunteer to take the burden off the shoulders of those in power. Be collaborative with your team. Make it a priority to help others succeed—be altruistic.

EQ (Emotional maturity)

Emotional Intelligence (EQ) has been around since Daniel Goleman crystalized the concept many years ago. Our take on EQ is more along the lines of emotional maturity. On the surface there seems to be a correlation between general intelligence and maturity. Some of us know people who are extremely bright but don't seem to be very mature emotionally. They are not comfortable in social interactions and don't seem to get the joke, often stating, "I don't get it." If you look a bit deeper, however, emotional intelligence (emotional maturity) and intelligence are not really related at all. Some of the funniest people we know are also the most intelligent, yet their humor is based on their insecurities and their inability to cope with emotionally charged situations. They are intellectually smart, but emotionally immature. Conflicts and frustrations can arise when people who live in the world of innuendo and humor try to communicate with those who are more serious. Conflicts can also crop up between people who are seen as emotionally immature (those who create drama) and those who prefer to keep their emotions in check.

There are many ways in which you can demonstrate an ability to recognize your own and others' emotions and to use emotions to guide your thinking and behavior. First, recognize when you don't know what you don't know. This may be shocking to you because you think it shows a sign of weakness. It actually is a sign of strength to recognize you may not know something and to express a willingness to learn. The same goes for knowing when to ask for help. You demonstrate the ability to be resourceful when doing so. Kindness and compassion, when demonstrated, are powerful influencers. Remember our Radiator discussion. People who demonstrate kindness and compassion toward others are empathetic and emotionally mature. Another indicator of emotional maturity is knowing when to "cool down" in between feeling and reacting. The cool down period allows you to think about how you want to react in a tough situation. Over time, this cooling off period will get shorter and shorter. Your reaction to something will be more thoughtful and mindful, and your words will be composed and devoid of high emotions. These are just some ways in which you can change your direction from a purely emotional reaction to exhibiting emotional maturity and smartness.

Conflict styles

As with personality styles, conflict styles can also create tension and interfere with effective outcomes.

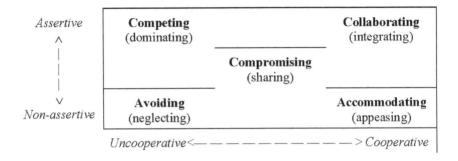

If you look at the Thomas-Kilmann Conflict Mode material, you will note that there are two intersecting scales they talk about: Assertiveness and Cooperativeness. You can be high or low on either scale. When you cross both scales, you have five theoretical conflict/fighting styles. As you can see from the graphic, you can have a conflict style that is either *Collaborating, Competing, Avoiding, Accommodating,* or *Compromising.* And, like toxic personality relationships, it is difficult to deal with opposing conflict styles. It is hard, for example, to resolve issues when one person is overly competitive while their discussion partner just wants to walk away from the discussion, or when one person wants a compromise while the other just wants to win.

Take stock of where you are and in what direction you are heading. You will inevitably be faced with the choice of different styles to employ depending on the circumstances with which you are faced. It is the style you consciously apply that can alter the outcome of the situation or your prospects for mitigating or resolving conflict.

Power and influence

Simply put, the person who is the most versatile is the person with the most power, regardless of personality, style, or title. A leader may have position power based on their job title, but young adults know as well as anyone that "title power" means little in terms of getting the results any organization seeks. Those who you are willing to follow, those with true organizational power and the power to influence others, are the people who are able to meet the needs of others and who can vary their communication approach in order to be altruistic.

Help others perform at an optimal level of stress

It is one thing to keep abreast of where you are and the direction in which you are heading. You will distinguish yourself from others if you help bring others along, particularly in conflict situations. Conflict causes stress and while a certain amount of healthy stress (eustress) is needed to combat apathy, too much stress (distress) provides the match that sets conflict on fire. Here are some things you can do to help others:

- Help others establish clear job responsibilities, standards of performance, and level of authority
- Agree upon goals/objectives
- Share work goals and emphasize the significance of their performance to successful outcomes

- Seek and get feedback regularly
- Encourage open communication
- Give positive feedback when merited
- Listen
- Help maintain a sense of self-dignity
- Expect improved performance
- Model desired performance
- When performance is negative, critique the performance and not the person
- Speak in a gentle but confident tone

Chapter 9

Man Overboard: What to Do When You're in Trouble

Mentoring/Coaching

Many people in leadership positions obtain (or keep) their position/credibility because they have sought the assistance of a coach. People seek a coach for a myriad of reasons. They may feel stuck in their career and need help getting to the next level. Or maybe a person is deciding whether to change direction in their field or wants to switch to an entirely different industry or expertise. They might be dealing with a particularly challenging situation or colleague, or they may simply need guidance navigating a new position, a new leadership role, or a skill that they haven't yet mastered. It is always good to have a clear understanding of why you are seeking a coach.

A coaching relationship can be informal or formal. The coach is someone who will listen to your issues and offer advice or an empathetic ear. The coach could be someone in authority or a willing colleague/friend who acts as a mirror to your concerns and ideas so you can hear what you are actually saying. The coaching process allows you to test out your thoughts before acting upon them; it's a check on your judgment and intuition. It's a two-way, mutually beneficial process; most coaches we've spoken to have learned as much from the person they are coaching as the person learned from them. That's one of the reasons that we encourage people to coach another person. For your own personal/professional growth, we highly recommend that you seek out a coach of your own. Once, while conducting a leadership workshop at a large corporation, just out of curiosity, Harvey asked the participants how many people had an organizational coach of their own. Nearly all the people raised their hands.

Potential Termination

If you ever feel that your job is in jeopardy (in all honesty, there may be many days throughout your career when you feel that your job is in jeopardy but often that is the fear factor kicking in), you should seek counsel (not necessarily a lawyer) to get a reality check on the situation and to either put together an effective strategy for salvaging your job or to develop an exit strategy. That does not always prove to be successful but it gives you a chance to talk through the situation with an expert and it is a great channel for your frustration, anger, and disappointment.

When Mara counsels clients in this regard, she aims to get them to be more objective and to see the situation as it really exists. She empowers them to deal effectively through a well-thought-out plan of action and a script. How many of you were in a fraternity or sorority? While hazing is something that is not condoned on campuses today, let's face it, hazing goes on. And a type of it goes on in the workplace. Sexual harassment and discrimination are behaviors that are wrong and unlawful and companies can be exposed to serious liability for such conduct. Ther are other types of conduct by seasoned leaders that may be misguided (not illegal). Such conduct is meant to instill in junior people the rigor needed to be the best they can be in their chosen field. It is meant to increase group loyalty, but are there any other positives? Well, it causes you to acquire some degree of self-doubt leading you to question yourself about whether you are working as hard as you can, meeting as many deadlines as you can, delivering the best work product that you can, achieving the most potential as you can, pleasing the most clients and customers as you can, having the best social interactions with others as you can and so on. It really is one of the many ways we go in the work world, as Jim Collins once said, "from good to great."

Chapter 10

Conclusion

Home Port

In this book, we have tried to lay out practical advice to help young adults (a) gain entry into the world of work, (b) understand and reduce the expectations gap between young workers and their employers in order to establish a firm footing within a company, and (c) develop strategies for successfully influencing and leading others as your career progresses. We've given valuable tips and examples of what works and what doesn't. This book is not designed for readers to read once and put back on the shelf. It is meant to be a reference guide that the reader will use as a "career companion," a behavioral manual on how to maximize your potential in the world of work.

Through our personal and professional experiences with young adults, we know that the work world is and will continue to be a better place than the work world in which we commenced our careers simply because of all the strengths you bring to it. Young adults today possess enormous strengths that, we believe, will only enhance the work world over time. Young adults possess a quest for purpose and meaning in their work. Looking back to our peer group when we were building our careers, we don't know too many boomer generation folks who stopped to think about or question whether they derived meaning and purpose from their work. This ubiquitous quest for meaning among young adults is causing companies to better articulate their corporate missions and engage in purposeful social responsibility and community service. Young adults are confident when questioning why things are done the way they have been done in the past. Many companies are engaging in this process of questioning which encourages critical evaluation of existing methods and processes. As a result of this introspective approach, the groundwork is being laid for potential change and innovation in companies from which you will benefit.

Young adults want to succeed and do a good job. You ask for feedback and direction because you want to excel at the tasks you've been assigned. Companies today recognize that and are training managers to have more face-to-face encounters specifically for feedback. Your technology savviness is so vast that many companies are relying on their young adult hires to bring them into the 21st century in order to leverage opportunities by using social media and digital marketing. You are resourceful with the ability to find answers at the push of a button. There is nothing you can't figure out when put to the test. What a huge advantage this asset presents for a company. Young adults' enthusiasm in the pursuit of their endeavors is infectious and can be a great asset for a company's overall culture. Young adults are transparent in that you readily share your thoughts, feelings, and concerns and that tranparency is going to make companies more accountable, purposeful and open. You don't like and will not tolerate bad actors. Ultimately, it is our hope that the work place will be a kinder, more empathic environment because of this quality that you possess. So, you see, there are many strengths and qualities you bring to the work world that are positive and will, in our view, cause the work world to be a better place over time. But you need to understand that your strengths, enlightened thinking, points of view and perspective may make members of other generations in the workplace uncomfortable at first. Therefore, it is incumbent upon you to do your part to reduce the expectations gap and be more adaptable and sensitive to the way businesses work and the views of others. This book, we hope, will be a reference guide for you throughout your career journey and different chapters may be relevant at different times in that journey.

All of this advice said, we encourage you to start with a serious look in the mirror to find out who you really are, identify what value you can bring to the organization, and where you want to be in the future. At times, the waters may be rough. But, with smart planning, help from others, self-insight, and a bit of opportunistic luck, you will be able to reach your destination safe and sound.

About the Authors

Mara spent eighteen years at the international law firm of White & Case LLP, where she was Counsel to the Firm and practiced employment law. At White & Case, Mara was actively involved in recruiting and in Equal Employment Opportunity and Diversity programs, and was a member of the firm's Women Lawyers' Network Committee. Mara's human resources operational experience included Deloitte Services LP where she was Chief of Staff to the National Director of Human Resources and Chief Operating Officer for the Retention and Advancement of Women. In addition, she held senior positions at Starwood Capital Group, a worldwide real estate private equity company, and KSL Media, Inc., an independent media agency, where she served as full-time consultant acting as Human Resources Director. In April 2009, Mara formed WISE HR Strategies LLC in order to provide institutional-firm-quality services at one-third the cost to clients needing strategic and operational human resources and employment law advice. WISE HR Strategies' clients include for-profit and not-for-profit institutions and senior level executives. Mara is admitted to practice law in the State of New York.

Mara also sits on several advisory boards. She is a member of the

Board of Observers of Muhlenberg College where she is charged with advising the President and Board of Trustees on areas of improvement. She is a member of the Director's Advisory Council of the Dartmouth-Hitchcock Norris Cotton Cancer Center, where she advises the director of the cancer center across the range of the director's responsibilities in the areas of operational and strategic matters.

Mara has had several entrepreneurial endeavors that include founding an organization, Second Shift®, in 1998. Second Shift's® mission is to provide a forum and resource center for career women who devote themselves to their careers, the care of their families, and the employers who employ them. The forum and resource center provide opportunities for networking, education, socializing, and sharing ideas and strategies toward finding and maintaining a balance between family and work obligations. Second Shift® has had over 600 participants, including career women from all industries with children of all ages. The organization sponsored live educational events featuring distinguished guest speakers on topics relevant to career moms and moms seeking reentry into the workforce and live networking events to further their business and community contacts and opportunities. Mara graduated from Muhlenberg College with a B.A. in Industrial and Organizational Behavior and she received her J.D. from Fordham University School of Law.

Harvey Robbins, president of Robbins & Robbins, Inc. located in Minnetonka, Minnesota, has been a practicing business psychologist since 1974. His broad experience provides his clients with training in leadership skills, management skills, team leadership skills, high performance team building, as well as consulting in leadership effectiveness, team effectiveness, change management, interpersonal influence, and executive coaching.

Harvey has provided international consulting services to numerous corporations and federal and state agencies including the U.S. Treasury ATF, American Express, AT&T, Allied Signal, FMC, General Dynamics, Honeywell, 3M, IRS, International Multifoods, Johnson & Johnson, Southern Company, Target Stores, Toro, US West, Winnebago, Upsher-Smith Laboratories, U.S. Secret Service, and U.S. Customs. He has also presented at many national and international conferences.

Prior to 1982, Robbins worked as a Personnel Research Psychologist for the psychological services branch of the intergovernmental personnel programs division of the U.S. Civil Service Commission (CIA), as a Manager of Personnel Development and Research for Burlington Northern, Inc., and as a Corporate Manager of Organization Development for Honeywell.

Harvey currently is a Fellow of Executive Education at the Carlson School of Management at the University of Minnesota.

Harvey, a native of New York City, received his doctorate in clinical psychology from A&M-Commerce. He is the author of seven books *Turf Wars: Moving from Competition to Collaboration, How to Speak and Listen Effectively, Why Teams Don't Work, Why Change Doesn't Work, The New Why Teams Don't Work, Transcompetition,* and a newly released book entitled *The Accidental Leader. Why Teams Don't Work,* co-authored with newspaper business columnist Michael Finley, received the 1995 Financial Times / Booz Allen & Hamilton Global Business Book Award. *Transcompetition,* also with Michael Finley, was published as a lead book with McGraw-Hill's new Business Week Books division in 1998. He is currently working on a book tentatively titled *Why People Don't Get Along.*

The Authors' Pitches

MARA

Let me tell you a little about myself. At fourteen, I asked my dad, a doctor, if he had a patient who could give me a job in personnel. Strangely, I knew at the ripe age of fourteen that I wanted to combine my interests in people and business. I ended up at Eagle Pencil Factory working in their labor relations department for my high school internship. Thereafter, I went to Muhlenberg College where I self-designed a major: Industrial and Organizational Behavior. I graduated in a year of a major recession and because of that recession, there were no jobs in personnel or HR, which was the new, sexy name for the field. Desperate to start working, I took a job in sales, selling temperature measurement devices. Eight months in, I hated it and took my father's suggestion and applied to law school. I went to law school at night while working full time as a law clerk for a major accounting firm. After getting my law degree, I began work at White & Case, an international Wall Street law firm where I worked my way up the ladder to Counsel. After eighteen years, I left big firm practice and held senior level human resources roles for companies in the professional services, private equity, and media industries. In 2009, I started my own employment law and HR advisory practice where I represent for profits, nonprofits, and senior executives on every topic related to employment.

In 2011, Harvey and I developed SharpenUrEdge™ training for

young adults entering the workplace. My strengths are that I possess high energy, which results in strong output in everything I do. I accomplish my goals, I am adaptable to different situations and people, and I am a very strong communicator and collaborator. My husband, Rich, is a private equity investor and together we have two sons—Gabriel, who recently graduated from Middlebury College where he was a student athlete (goalie varsity lacrosse) and works for the investment bank, Goldman Sachs, and Noah, a sophomore at Hamilton College, also a goalie for his varsity lacrosse team. In my free time, I am a long-distance swimmer, skier, hiker, sailor, and golfer, and I love to entertain.

HARVEY

I was born and raised in the Bronx, New York. Arrested at eight for gang fighting (my mother brought me into that lifestyle ... it was her gang), I was given a choice of going to juvie (juvenile detention) or joining the PAL (police athletic league) and learning to shoot real weapons. Naturally, I joined the PAL and shot through elementary school, high school, and college. I studied physics at Polytechnic Institute of Brooklyn and switched to psychology for my masters and doctorate at Texas A&M – Commerce. After graduation, I was recruited by the Psychological Services Division of the Intergovernmental Personnel Programs Division of the U.S. Civil Service Commission, which, it turns out, was a cover for doing individual and organizational assessments as a psychologist for the CIA, a kind of mind manipulation so to speak (shhh!!). They also sent me to sniper school because of my shooting background.

After four years, I was transferred to Minneapolis where I worked for the organization for a year until I was recruited to work as Manager of Personnel and Research for Burlington Northern. After three years, I was recruited to be Manager of Organization Development at Honeywell. After another three years, I left and started my own consultancy, Robbins & Robbins, providing consulting services and workshops on leadership, teamwork, change, and interpersonal influence. During this time, I wrote/co-wrote seven books on teamwork, leadership, and change (One, *Why Teams Don't Work*, won the Booze-Allan Hamilton/Financial Times Business Book of the Year for the Americas) and became a sculptor/artist while continuing to write books about subjects that made me angry.

After doing some executive coaching for Mara Weissmann's clients (I was referred to her by a mutual friend), I began working with her on SharpenUrEdge™ in 2011. Since we had a mutual interest in getting our Millennial boys into good schools and good jobs, the chance to build a useful system to accomplish this just made sense to me. Now, I continue to conduct workshops and sit around writing more books and working on my "art." My wife of thirty-five years, Nancy, is a senior executive at Ameriprise Financial after serving as an executive at Target for over twenty years. My son, Max, graduated from the University of Wisconsin, is married, and has a great job.

Acknowledgments

We'd like to thank Peter Young and Erica Ellis for formatting and editing. A big thank you to Allison Motola for the graphic art cover design. Many family and friends have read our manuscript and provided us with insightful comments. A big shout out goes to friends, Michael Crane and Sharon Holand Gelfand for their keen eye and enthusiasm for our project and Gabe Weissmann and Madelaine Levey who read our manuscript on the eve of starting their first, full-time jobs and said it was "incredibly helpful" as they begin this new, exciting chapter in their lives.

Endnotes

[i] Locke, John Blog, Manager, Freelock, LLC, with permission by author to reprint.

[ii] Murphy, Mark, CEO of Leadership IQ, *"Hiring for Attitude: Research and Tools to Skyrocket Your Success Rate,"* (2102).

[iii] Bradberry, Travis and Greaves, Jean, *"Emotional Intelligence 2.0,"* (TalentSmart 2009).

[iv] Williams, David, K., *Why You Should Fill Your Company With 'Athletes,' Entrepreneurs, Forbes* (October 2, 2013).

[v] Ibid.

[vi] Alsop, Ron, *"The Trophy Kids' Go to Work,"* Wall Street Journal (Oct. 21, 2008.)

[vii] White, Marion PhD, *"Rethinking Generation Gaps in the Workplace: Focus on Shared Values,"* (2011).

[viii] *"How College Students Think They are More Special Than EVER: Study Reveals Rocketing Sense of Entitlement on U.S. Campuses,"* Daily Mail Reporter *(*January 5, 201).

[ix] Hofschneider, Anita, *"Bosses Say 'Pick Up the Phone,'"* The Wall Street Journal, (Aug. 27, 2013).

[x] Navarrette, Ruben, *"Are Millennials Cut Out for this Market,"* CNN.com (Aug. 5, 2011).

[xi] Davidson, Paul, *"Wanted Millennials Who Know How To Interview,"* USA Today (April 29, 2013).

[xii] Costello, Michelle, *"Millennials Are the Most Stressed Out Generation,"* NBC News (February 11, 2013).

[xiii] Stein, Joel, *"The Me Me Me Generation,"* TIME.com (May 20, 2013).

[xiv] Greenburg, O'Malley Zack, *"How Millennials Can Survive This Economy,"* TODAY.com (November 30, 2011).

[xv] Friedman, Thomas, *"Need a Job? Invent It,"* The New York Times (May 30, 2013).

[xvi] Dominus, Susan, *"How to Get a Job with a Philosophy Degree,"* The New York Times Magazine (September 13, 2013).

[xvii] Quenqua, Douglas, *"Seeing Narcissists Everywhere,"* The New York Times (August 5, 2013).

[xviii] Seymour, *Lesley Jane, "How I Hire: 6 Ways I Find and Hire Hardworking Millennials,"* LinkedIn (September 24, 2013).

[xix] Merryman, Ashley, *"Losing is Good For You,"* The New York Times (September 24, 2013).

[xx] Hofschneider, Anita, *"Should You Bring Mom and Dad to the Office?"* Wall Street Journal (September 10, 2013).

[xxi] Urban, *Tim, "Why Generation Y Yuppies are Unhappy,"* Huffingtonpost.com (September 9, 2013).

[xxii] Tugend, Alina *"Just Graduated, and Fumbling Through a First Job,"* The New York Times (April 4, 2014).

[xxiii] Shulevitz, Judith, *"Hiding From Scary Ideas: Do Students Really Need Cookies and Play-Doh to Deal with the Trauma of Listening to Unpopular Opinions?"* The New York Times (March 21, 2015) .

[xxiv] Levine, Madeline, *"Raising Successful Children,"* The New York Times (August 4, 2012).

[xxv] Quenqua, Douglas, *"Seeing Narcissists Everywhere,"* The New York Times (August 5, 2013).

[xxvi] Twenge, Jean, PhD, *GenerationMe,* (Atria Books 2006).

[xxvii] Twenge, Jean PhD and Keith Campbell, *"The Narcissism Epidemic"* (Free Press 2009).

[xxviii] Quenqua, Douglas, *"Seeing Narcissists Everywhere,"* The New York Times (August 5, 2013).

[xxix] *GenerationMe,* page 26.

[xxx] Ibid, page 27.

[xxxi] Ibid. page 29.

[xxxii] Ibid. page 31.

[xxxiii] Ibid. page 37.

[xxxiv] Ibid. page 40.

xxxv "Perfect Storm." Wikipedia: The Free Encyclopedia. Wikimedia Foundation, Inc. (Andrew Stern 1-1-2008).

xxxvixxxvi Clarke, Suzan, *"8-Year Old Gets Catastrophe Award for Most Homework Excuses,"* ABC Good orning America, May 29, 2012.

xxxvii Dweck, Carol PhD, *"Mindset: How You Can Fulfill Your Potential"* (Ballantine Books 2007).

xxxviii Levine, Madeline, *"The Price of Privilege"* (HarperCollins 2006).

xxxix Deloitte White Paper, *"Connecting Across the Generations in the Workplace."*

xl Tugend, Anita, *"Just Graduated, and Fumbling Through a First Job,"* The New York Times, April 4, 2014.

xli State Risk Management News (Tristatepeo.com) Study (2010).

xlii Balderrama, Anthony, *"Generation Y: Too Demanding at Work?"* Careerbuilder.com (2007).

xliii EdGlossary.org, definition of *Rubric* (August 29, 2013).

xliv Alsop, Ron, *"The 'Trophy Kids' Go to Work,"* The Wall Street Journal, Oct. 21, 2008.

xlv Hansen, Randall S., PhD, *"Pereption vs. Reality: 10 Truths About Generation Y Workforce,"* (Quintessential Careers).

xlvi Graves, Jada, *"Millennial Workers: Entitled, Needy, Self- Centered,"* U.S. World & News Report, (June 27, 2012).

xlvii Newport, Cal, *"Follow a Career Passion? Let It Follow You,"* The New York Times (September 29, 2012).

xlviii Meister, Jeanne, *"Job Hopping Is the 'New Normal' for Millennials: Three Ways to Prevent a Human Resource Nightmare,"* Forbes (August 14, 2012) .

xlix Ibid.

l Pink, Daniel, *"A Whole New Mind,"* (Riverhead Books 2005), pgs. 51-52.

li Hansen, Randall S., PhD, *"Pereption vs. Reality: 10 Truths About Generation Y Workforce,"* (Quintessential Careers).

[lii] https://en.wikipedia.org/wiki/**Pre-mortem**Wikipedia.

[liii] Hofschneider, Anita, *"Bosses Say 'Pick Up the Phone,'"* The Wall Street Journal (August 27, 2013).

[liv] Watkins, Michael, *"The First 90 Days: Critical Success Strategies for New Leaders at All Levels,"* (Harvard Business School Press 2003).

[lv] Neilson, Gary, Pasternack, Bruce and Van Nuys, Karen, *"The Passive-Aggressive Organization,"* Harvard Business Review, (October 2005).

[lvi] Emerson, Richard M., Social Exchange Theory, *"Annual Review of Sociology,"*
Vol. 2 (1976); Törnblom, Kjell, Kazemi, Ali, *"The Handbook of Social Resources Theory: Theoretical Extensions, Empirical Insights, and Social Applications."* (Springer-Verlag New York 2012).

[lvii] Ross, Judith, *"How to Ask Better Questions,"* Harvard Business Review, May 6, 2009.

[lviii] Urban, Tim, *"Why Generation Y Yuppies are Unhappy,"* Huffingtonpost.com, (September 9, 2013).

[lix] www.sailo.com.

[lx] Buckingham, Jane and Buckingham, Marcus, *"Note to Gen Y Workers: Performance on the Job Actually Matters,"* Time Magazine, (September 28, 2012).

[lxi] http://www.merriam-webster.com/dictionary/self-awareness

[lxii] Merrill, David W. and Reid, Roger H. *"Personal Styles and Effective Performance,"* (Chilton Book Company 1981).

[lxiii] CPP Global Human Capital Report, *"Workplace Conflict and How Businesses can Harness it to Thrive"* (July 2008).

[lxiv] Schmidt, Jeff, *"Bad Bosses: What Kind are You?"* BusinessWeek (January 26, 2010).

[lxv] O'Brien, Sue, Personal Story.

[lxvi] wikipedia.org, Psychological Projection, Wikipedia

[lxvii] Strategic Direction, trainingontarget.com, *Study on Versatility* (2012).

Printed in the USA
CPSIA information can be obtained
at www.ICGtesting.com
CBHW031320040924
14106CB00031B/184